The* Spoken word Revolution

The* SPOKEN word ReVOLUTiON

(slam, hip hop & the poetry
of a new generation)

edited by **mark eleveld**
advised by **marc smith**
introduction by **billy collins,**
u.s. poet laureate

**sourcebooks
mediaFusion**

An Imprint of Sourcebooks Inc.®
Naperville, Illinois

Published by Sourcebooks, Inc.

P.O. Box 4410, Naperville, Illinois 60567-4410

(630) 961-3900

FAX: (630) 961-2168

www.sourcebooks.com

Hardcover edition was cataloged as follows:

The spoken word revolution : slam, hip hop, and the poetry of a new generation / [edited by] Mark Eleveld and Marc Smith.

     p. cm.

     1. American poetry—20th century. 2. Performance art—United States. 3. American poetry—21st century. 4. Oral interpretation of poetry. 5. Hip-hop—Poetry. 6. Sound poetry. I. Eleveld, Mark. II. Smith, Marc.

    PS615.S65 2003

    811'.508—dc21

                            2003000841

Printed and bound in the United States of America

BG   10 9 8 7 6 5 4 3 2

To "So What"...
Thank You, Marc.

contents

CD

Note from the Publisher

When Sourcebooks MediaFusion published *Poetry Speaks* in the fall of 2001, the overwhelming reception to that book-and-audio-CD compilation opened up a world of possibilities for this publisher. One of the immediate outcomes of that success was the opportunity to work with Mark Eleveld and Marc Smith on *The Spoken Word Revolution*. Where *Poetry Speaks* focused on historic poets whose work long ago became part of the canon, *Spoken Word* delves into the living, churning, vibrant world of one of today's most widespread and acclaimed forms of poetry—spoken word.

Spoken word encompasses many movements, yet they all share a common credo—namely, that their poetry is designed to be performed in front of an audience. While no one could claim to have the "definitive" collection of slam, hip hop, and other spoken word styles—the art form is still kicking, breathing, and evolving—this book aims to introduce you to the art with a diverse array of extraordinary talent.

As with any art form that places oral performance at its core, it is essential that you hear the performances, which is why we've included a seventy-five-minute audio CD narrated by slam founder Marc Smith. The spoken word movement recognizes that to be a vital, relevant part of our culture, poetry must spread beyond the classroom and reach people where they live. Poetry was originally an oral art form—and a popular one. Spoken word returns to poetry's roots, and we revel in the opportunity to be a part of today's revolution.

CD track list

They sat at the panel, the learned and poetic, some with their credentials resting high upon their shoulders. The one who was least important in these "academic" terms, however, was being interviewed the most. He was holding his hands in front of him, pushing his straight jawbone out while smiling with a bravado that he had held fast for over a decade— trying to do what few before him, if any, had done. And while he was very successful in what he created in his world of poetry, he felt uncomfortable in these surroundings.

The other gentleman was smartly dressed, with dark tie and Wall Street blazer. He spoke well, was enthusiastic with his back-handed compliments, and was receptive to the open adulation given to him by the others on the panel. After all, he had been handed the current editorship to the world's premier poetry magazine, and that meant something. Another member of the panel, a former Pulitzer Prize winner and poet laureate commented, "It is something you dream about," in regards to getting published by this same magazine. Together, this group of poets—save one— who sounded as if they had just gotten off the Concorde from Paris, began name-dropping Ivy League pretensions and Nobel Prize winner mentorships, all highlighting the excitement of being published by this "King Maker" of poetic magazines. All but one rehashed positive stories about this institution, the smartly dressed man even going so far as to say, "Most of it [the poetry] is pretty awful...but if it is good, we catch it. That is what we do." The other man continued to sit there quietly, understanding the put-down as just that. He was Chicago tough, and this aristocratic bullshit was just one more thing being pushed in his face.

Finally, after the premise of the show was built and the characters identified, John Callaway, the famous, old, white-haired Chicago broadcaster—the one who looked like everyone's grandfather—went to work. He pointed at the former construction worker, now poet inventor, and said, "You were kind of a smartass about it, weren't you? We shouldn't mince words here. You two," he glanced at the smartly dressed man, "weren't in love with each other."

"I wasn't a smartass about it at first. I held the magazine in high reverence. My first rejections came from the magazine. I'd tack them up to the refrigerator, until it was full…."

Callaway had dealt with some of the best Chicago figures: Mike Royko, Studs Terkel, the Daleys. He kept driving Marc. "When did you first start writing poetry?"

"When I was nineteen."

"How many years did you send poems to the magazine?"

"Sixteen." And although it wasn't stated out loud, sixteen years of rejections said something very clearly. After all, the panel had already established that good poems didn't slip through this magazine. So what does that say about his writing? His writing for the last sixteen years, no less! What didn't he have that all the other poets on the panel did?

"You see," Marc Smith began, on a paraphrased moment of why he created Poetry Slams, "you had to get in, get in," his head directed to the other side of the panel, the haves. "And I was an outsider…and I thought I had something to say, like a lot of outsiders do. There were a lot of people snubbing me who shouldn't have been snubbing me. So I just ended up doing it my own way, like a lot of people do…." He became more important to poetry than any other on the panel. He created a revolution.

A couple of years later, this same self-made Chicago poet was being interviewed on *60 Minutes*, the most famous weekly news program in the world.

"When I started, nobody wanted to go to poetry readings. Slam gave it life…a community where you didn't have to be a special something, feel bad that you weren't educated a special way…I think when poetry went from the oral tradition to the page, someone should've asked, is that really poetry? I think slam gets poetry back to its roots, breathing life into the words."

Morley Safer poked a little deeper, and asked about the makeup of the slam competition. What about this giving of numbers to poems?

"Totally absurd," smiled Marc.

Poems on the page, Poems in the air

(by Billy Collins, U.S. Poet Laureate)

In recent decades, the phenomenon of the poetry reading has become as much a regular part of our cultural menu as the chamber music recital or the film festival. Readings are taking place at colleges and libraries, bars and coffee shops, bookstores, galleries, and at least one Laundromat that I've heard of. In some cases, a handful of devotees form a ritual semicircle around the poet, but there are also mega-readings attended by hordes, notably the Sunken Garden readings in Connecticut that boast audiences of up to three thousand, enough to cause "poetry traffic jams." Then, of course, there is the mother of all poetry pow-wows, the Dodge Festival, a biennial four-day event in Waterloo Village, New Jersey, that attracts more than ten thousand people each year. It is likely that at this very minute, somewhere in the world, someone is standing behind a podium with a handful of poems, tentatively tapping a microphone with one finger, preparing to lift poetry off the page and into the air. What is the draw? Why insist on being in the presence of an author when we have already met him at his best? Why not submit to our print culture and stay home with a cup of tea—or a few inches of whiskey—and open a book?

For one thing, the poetry reading offers a double connection: one with the poet who stands up from the page and delivers, and another with the audience united by a common interest. Insofar as poems are composed by the ear, they are designed to be heard as well as read. To hear a poem is to experience its momentary escape from the prison cell of the page, where silence is enforced, to a freedom dependent only on the ability to open the mouth—that most democratic of instruments—and speak.

Another reason may lie in the oral reading's ability to return readers to a time preceding the dominance of print, when a new dimension of silence (and a new dimension of loneliness according to Marshall MacLuhan) was added to the experience of verbal communication. To sit in a room with others and witness a breathing poet saying his or her own poem aloud provides a relief from the isolation of print, not to mention more existential feelings of estrangement. In the reading, poet and audience are bodily exposed to one another and take on the visibility they mutually lack in the silent transaction of the page. In this light, the public reading is a throwback, a resurrection of the Romantic notions of spontaneity and genius as opposed to the modernist sense of the author as a reclusive inscriber of verbal patterns or, more extremely, the postmodernist sense of the author as a false construction, the fond illusion of old-fashioned readers.

These days, when academic discourse wants to replace the warmth of voice with the chilliness of text, hearing a poem said out loud reminds us of the spoken origins of poetry and the communal nature of the exchange. Poetry readings would not be so popular if these gains did not offset the possible misalignments that can be part of the experience: like the eerie feeling a poet might have when surrounded by strangers who seem to know his or her secrets and the almost inevitable failure of the author—the one with the bad tie and worse table manners—to match the audience's original encounter with him or her in discreet lines of verse. The public reading may convey the dramatic illusion that the words are issuing forth directly from the source, as if the poem were not merely being recited but spontaneously composed on the spot. The vocal poet is an echo of the Orphic singer, the embodiment of the ancient lyric impulse. The reading of a poem out loud turns authorship into a performance, as commentator Peter Middleton put it, and may even be said to "re-establish the authority of authorship in the face of its downsizing by the academic industry." So, hearing a poem lends the experience of literature an immediacy, a reality not found on the page where we must conjure up the ghost-form of the poet who wrote the poems.

Billy Collins

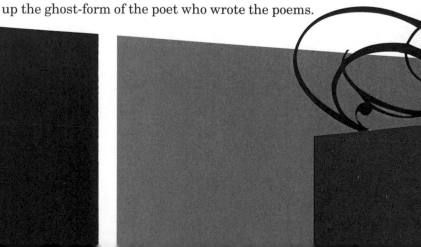

Eamon Grennan recently told me that he often follows the reading of a poem in his workshop with the question "Is anybody there?" That is, do you hear in the poem a voice speaking, through which the presence of another person can be easily inferred? The orally delivered poem brings to us the sound and idiolect of a person's voice, a quality often muffled between the covers of a book or intentionally obliterated by poets who seek a purity of language rinsed of human speech.

What the live reading and the recorded reading provide, then, is voice. Surely, we hear an inner voice when we hold a book of poetry in our hands and read in silence, but it is not the voice of the poet. Rather, it is our own internal voice that claims the poem. The intimacy of poetry even allows us to feel that we have replaced the poet just as we replace the singer—and even the composer if we care to—when we sing along with the radio in a car. A dependable sign that you like a poem is the pleasurable feeling that you are actually inventing it as you read it. Further, the immediacy of a live reading extends to the listener a degree of participation. Paying attention approaches being a creative act when we realize that the poem is being enacted beyond our control—the control we exercise with a text by pausing, rereading, and skipping. Yet there is a pleasurable passivity in listening. We submit to the pace of the reader who governs the experience; we relax into a state of acceptance not common to reading—we can even close our eyes. Also, in a live reading we lose the equilibrium of the typographical shape of the poem; the linebreaks and stanzas dissolve into pure sound. And as Philip Larkin pointed out, we cannot see the end of the poem coming and make preparations for it to be over. A reader walks at his own pace; a listener travels downhill by sled.

Listening to a poet read the poem, we may feel that he or she has repossessed the poem, taken it out of our heads and broadcast it to the world. But the poem also may seem refreshened, newly minted. When oral delivery is at its best, time flows in reverse. All the books containing the poem are returned to the warehouse; the printing press runs backward; the manuscript is mailed back to the poet who stands before us now with a page in his hand—the original sheet, let's say—and reads the poem as if for the very first time.

billy collins

*hear...
track 3

Introduction to Poetry

I ask them to take a poem
and hold it up to the light
like a color slide

or press an ear against its hive.

I say drop a mouse into a poem
and watch him probe his way out,

or walk inside the poem's room
and feel the walls for a light switch.

I want them to waterski
across the surface of a poem
waving at the author's name on the shore.

But all they want to do
is tie the poem to a chair with rope
and torture a confession out of it.

They begin beating it with a hose
to find out what it really means.

regie gibson

alchemy

PRONOUN / NOUN / PREPOSITION / NOUN
PRONOUN / NOUN / PREPOSITION / NOUN
PRONOUN / ADJECTIVE / VERB / NOUN / PREPOSITION / NOUN
NOUN / VERB / ADVERB / CONJUNCTION / ARTICLE / NOUN
PREPOSITION / PRONOUN / NOUN

this / eroticism / of / language
this / copulation / of / words
this / slow / burning / fuck / of / syllables
poetry / is / more / than / the / sum
of / its / parts

*

Regie Gibson

the beat remnants

(tracks 5–8)

introduction

In its purest form, in the classical mode in which it was created, poetry was used to remember stories. Homer was a blind storyteller. That's all. Forget everything else about poetry. When there wasn't any TV or radio, people like Homer were paid to come out and entertain. The fire would be ablaze, people would gather in a circle, together, glass in hand, listening to the stories that helped shape the world. But poetry has long been separated from this idea. Perhaps the story of today's poetry begins in Chicago in 1912.

Harriet Monroe was a world-shaker. A poet and writer herself, Monroe was angered by the poor reputation and treatment then given to modern poetry. On the heels of Victorianism's self-defeating homage to Romanticism, Harriet Monroe began *Poetry* magazine as a means of trying to shake up an otherwise sterile poetic world.

Of the new artists, Monroe, also an art critic for the *Chicago Tribune*, leaned upon Duchamp's *Nude Descending a Staircase*, and stated,

> They throw a bomb into the entrenched camp, give to American art a much needed shaking up....Either these pictures are good or they are not. If they are good, they will make their way in spite of objection...Better the wildest extravagance of the cubists than the lifeless works of certain artists who ridiculed them...They [the new artists] represent a search for new beauty, impatience with formulae, a reaching out toward the inexpressible, a longing for new versions of truth. (*A History of Poetry in Letters*, Parisi and Young, 2002, p. 19–29)

One can't help but think that she applied this same ethos to her new magazine. By reaching across the ocean to Ezra Pound, she was the first to publish T.S. Eliot, the old lion of modern poetry. And while others were trying to catch their breath, she went ahead and printed Sandburg's wildly obscene "Chicago," where talk of "painted woman under the gaslamps" and "hog butchers" made its presence known; this was not your grandmother's poetry. This poetry was gritty, real, and revolutionary.

Some have referred to the beginnings of *Poetry* magazine as a Chicago renaissance of poetry. Perhaps it would be better to say that this renaissance, although begun in Chicago, started a world movement. The list of contributors to the magazine is the same list of canonized modernist writers who are studied and worshipped today: Wallace Stevens, Amy Lowell, D.H. Lawrence, Elizabeth Bishop, Marianne Moore, James Joyce, William Carlos Williams, and others. This magazine created, out of a need for an artistic shake-up, a legendary institution. This begs the question, does every revolution begun inevitably become an institution?

As the success of *Poetry* magazine kept climbing into and beyond the world wars, the authors who were once heralded as the social revolutionaries, the "longing for a new version of truth" poets (as perceived by Harriet Monroe in her remark about Duchamp) began a different type of movement. No longer concentrating only on works, they became new in criticism, and with the example of Eliot at the forefront, the New Critics began to seize the reins of the poetic climate. New Criticism as an ideology wanted to separate work from artist. This new school of thought wanted to maintain that poems are well-constructed objects to be judged independent of anything else. In a way, the artists became the critics, the revolution an institution, and—quite simply—the young the old. Instead of art being an attempt to change social problems, or to evaluate the realities of existence, as modernism did, the value became the art in and of itself.

Politically, there were many motivations for this. The era of American art was turning toward a right-wing, corporate image. If art critiqued American society, it was seen as unpatriotic and possibly communist. Because of these labels, poetry quickly divorced from reality and moved into structure. The New Critics were safe and elitist, and they swept into the academy.
The question turned from,

"What does it mean to be human now?" to "What is a well-crafted poem?" No longer would Homer as entertainer and storyteller be as important as rhyme scheme and meter.

As every movement causes a reaction, the Beats were close to emerging. By the mid-'40s, Jack Kerouac had already set out on his antithetical approach to the sterility of the learned. Frustrated with the life of literature at Columbia, he chose to look for truth in the world instead of in predetermined books of the learned. Instead of rewriting thought, Kerouac looked to jazz as a model for his system of spontaneous prose: "first thought, best thought." Reversing the credo of the New Critics, he sought not to see what the poem *was*, but to see what life *is*, and reflect that beauty by creating the poem. A throwback to the Romantics, Kerouac's friend, poet Allen Ginsberg, looked for inspiration in William Blake and Walt Whitman, seeking cadence and oral utterance within the framework of the Biblical tradition. As a generalization, Beat writing tended to be about spiritual awareness, anti-material, and anti–"Ozzie and Harriet nuclear family." While TV was broadcasting two single beds in the rooms of Lucy and Desi, Ginsberg was testing the limits of sexuality, drugs, and expression. And more than any other link to the present-day era, Allen Ginsberg's 1956 Gallery Six reading of "Howl" leads into todays' performance poetry. Although not a direct link in terms of style, certainly the Beat readings were a seedling in the importance of reading poetry aloud.

Since only a couple true Beatniks are still around, it is important to look at the work of some of the writers who were participating, learning, reading aloud, and writing aloud around the times of the Beats. And as the Beats influenced them, and they the Beats, these writers so too have helped influence the next generation of readers and writers. From Beatnik hipsters, to Carnegie award–winning professors, to Iowa poet laureates, to teachers of Pulitzer Prize winners, to Guggenheim directors and beyond, this first group of poets have helped set the tone for a whole generation. As an example of this influence, look for an excerpt by poet Regie Gibson's (mentored by Kent Foreman) homage to Jimi Hendrix following Ed Hirsch's "The Burning of the Midnight Lamp."

quincy troupe, jr.

Poem for the Root Doctor of Rock n Roll

& it all came together on the mississippi river

chuck, you there riding the rocking-blue sound
    wave

duck-walking the poetry of hoodoo down

& you were the mojo-hand

of juju crowing, the gut-bucket news—running it
    down

for two records sold to make a penny

back in those first days, "majoring in mouth"—

a long, gone, lean lightning rod

picking the edge, charging the wires

of songs, huckle-buckling "roll over

beethoven," playing "devil's music," till white
    devils stole it from you

& called it their own, "rock n roll"

devils like elvis & pat boone

who never duck-walked back in the alley with
    you

& bo diddley, little richard & the fatman from new
    orleans

all y'all slapping down songs meaner than the
    smell

of toejam & rot-gut whiskey breath

back there, in them back rooms

of throw down

back there, here your song lyrics grew, like fresh
    corn

you, chuck berry, an authentic american genius
    of barbecue sauce

& deep fried catfish licks, jack-salmon guitar

honky-tonk rhythms

jangling warm, vibrating sounds, choo-chooing
    train

whistles fiddling & smoking down the tracks of
    the blues

motivating through "little queenie," "maybelline"

decked out in red on sarah & finney

alarms rolling off your whipping tongue

in the words of "johnny b. good"

you clued us in, back to the magical hookup of
    ancestors

their seamless souls threading your breath

their blood in your sluicing strut

& too much "monkey business," the reason for
    their deaths, cold & searing

your spirit reaching down to the bones of your
    roots
deep in the "show me" blood of missouri soil
your pruned, hawk-look, profiling
where you rode your white cadillac of words,
    cruising
the highways of languages (what we speak &
    hear even now)
breathing inside your cadences
you shaped & wheeled the music
duck-walking the length of the stage
duck-walked your zinging metaphors of everyday
slip-slide & strut, vibrating your hummingbird
    wings
your strumming style, the cutting edge
you were what was to come

so hail, hail, chuck berry, root doctor of "rock n
    roll"
authentic american genius
tonguing deep river syllables
hail, hail, chuck berry, laying down the motivating
    juju
you great, american, mojo hand

root doctor, spirit, of american, "rock n roll"

track 5

Chicago
—for Howlin Wolf

1.
The wind/blade cutting in
& out swinging in over the lake
slicing white foam from the tips
of delicate water fingers
that danced & weaved
under the sunken light/night;
this wind/blade was so sharp & cold
it'd cut a four-legged mosquito into fours
while a hungry lion slept on the wings of some
    chittlins
slept within the blues of a poem that was formin

We came in the sulphuric night drinkin old crow
while a buzzard licked its beak atop the head of a
    tricky nixon
while gluttonous daley ate hundreds of pigs that
    were his ego
while daddy-o played bop on the box
came to the bituminous breath of chicago
howling with three-million voices of pain

& this is the music;

the kids of chicago have eyes that are older
than the deepest pain in the world
& they run with bare feet over south/side streets
shimmering with shivers of glass
razors that never seem to cut their feet;
they dance in & out of traffic—
the friday night smells of fish
& hog maws, the scoobedoo
sounds of bo diddley

2.
These streets belong to the dues/payer
To the blues/player/drinking whiskey on
    satdaynight
muddy waters & the wolfman howlin smokestack
    lightning
how many more years down in the bottom
no place to go moaning for my baby
a spoonful of evil
back door man
all night long how many more years
down in the bottom built for comfort

*

Chicago

Because I am a patriot, I love this bitch
You dig?
This sprawling, bawdy breathtaking witch
This pig,
   Sometimes
     She has her moods
       So stoically endured by her black bastards
       She broods
   Sometimes
     She's lonely.
       Like shrouded Lincoln Park winter
         midnights.
       Like overclouded Tuesday 4:30 a.m.s
         In garish lights
    She's sad
Or she gets mad !
    In sudden fits of angry gray she rages,
    Fakes out the weatherman,
      Our scientific sages,
        And proudly claims
        The ownership of dirty names
          her children call her,
"You frigid bitch!"

"You whore"
"Mistress of the rich"
  "More"

  "Chi"?
I know her for a great American Janus
'Cause, once, I was a ghetto urchin
       Playing in her anus
         Tenement yards
         Dodging shards
           Of shattered spirits...

Once when I was green and even April showered,
           Seedling shaped,
She smiled
And then commanded me to that door in back,
   Explained to me this Crime of being black.
       I was deflowered,
            Raped!
So I balled up into a fist and hated,
Pounded upon the prison gates
     Until the rage abated,

Until the knuckles of my soul were mutilated
And difficult to clench
Now, when I recall the stench
Of stockyards festering in her armpits,
I do not scream.

You see, I love her.
I love her awesome sunrise hair
I love the wealth
She will not share
with me.

Still, I love her dirty feet.
Her skidrow and her Maxwell Street.
Listen to her sing
My God, in spring,
Chicago balls the populace.
Blows down Michigan Avenue
Moist warm caresses
Inverts the secretaries' dresses
And promises passionate summer
thunder storms
filled with phallic lightning bolts
And it is Good!
Standing up on her glittering clitoris

At State and Randolph sts.
'Cause there are art fairs
and book stores in Hyde Park,
The whores, the pimps, the sharks
That hunt on 39th.
Wells St. is a symphony of joints
And from The Point
You can see a Disneyland loop.
At night
A swarm of technicolor fireflies
And ragged velvet skies.
This is The Truth!
I love this faithless bitch
That robbed me of my youth
But I will leave her,
Blow
And I will miss her when I go,
But I've got to...

*

george david miller

Before I Read
This Poem

Before I read this poem, I want to tell you some
    things
About myself.

I know—I'm like you
I can't stand this confessional poetry crap
The inner recesses of the soul and all that.
I think the more you say
The more you hide from others and from
    yourself.
Nietzsche said nobody ever wrote an authentic
Autobiography.

My life isn't a poem
It's a clearance sale at Wal-Mart
Buying all the Easter stuff
At half price
The week after the big rock is supposed
To have been moved from the cave.

While I'm always late for big sales,
I'm always right on time for the trivial things of life:
Mowing the lawn
Picking up the kids at soccer

Making sure the bras are snapped before they're
    placed in
The washer
Buying tampons with half-price coupons.

I always feel like I'm a relief pitcher
In the bullpen
Waiting and waiting and waiting
To get into the big game
For the big moment
But that big game
And that big moment
Don't come for me.

Or I'm the kid playing Candy Land
Who gets all the way to Ice Cream
At the top of the board
And then gets the Candy Canes card
And has to go back to the beginning.

My life is an endless series
Of trivial foreplay
It's like those advertisements
For the abdominal wheel

That is supposed to give you a six pack
Like Adonis
But two months after you bought it
Ends up in the garage as a replacement wheel
For your wheelbarrow.
Or it's like those religions
That tell us to look inside of ourselves
And we'll find the kingdom of God
But when we look inside ourselves
Which we always imagine to be
A golden chateau in the clouds
All we find is a raised ranch
In Bolingbrook.
It's like the glistening glamorous
Face on the barstool
At the beginning of the evening
That by the end of the evening
Is a mirage of mascara
Dirty rivulets streaming down
Her cheeks.
Or it's like the vociferous promises
Of politicians
Becoming the casual compromises of
Diluted legislation.
It's like the beautiful rooms
On Home and Garden television
That you try to emulate
But end up having
Someone finish for you.

The big moments of life are not:
When the walls of Jericho tumble
When Haley's Comet sparkles across the sky
When a knockout punch fells a fighter
Or when Sissyphus' boulder finally goes over the
     hill.

The big moments of life
Are not when the boulder clears the ridge
But when we tie our shoes
Spit on our hands
Take deep breaths
Flex our muscles
Focus all our energy
And do it all over again

Realizing
Each moment is history
Each moment is passion
Each action is meaning

With Big Mac breath
Tide scented clothes
And a Wal-Mart fanny pack
We can still raise our arms
To the heavens and scream
"I have lived, I have lived"—
Carving epic lives
From ordinary moments.

And that is the whole meaning of life
To be able to look to the heavens
And scream "I have lived, I have lived"—
To have carved epic lives
From ordinary moments.

This is my life—and it's your life too
This is my poem—and it's your poem too.
And you still don't know me
And I still don't know myself.

I Am Going to Start Living Like a Mystic

Today I am pulling on a green wool sweater
and walking across the park in a dusky snowfall.

The trees stand like twenty-seven prophets
   in a field,
each a station in a pilgrimage—silent, pondering.

Blue flakes of light falling across their bodies
are the ciphers of a secret, an occultation.

I will examine their leaves as pages in a text
and consider the bookish pigeons, students of
   winter.
I will kneel on the track of a vanquished squirrel
and stare into a blank pond for the figure of
   Sophia.
I will begin scouring the sky for signs
as if my whole future were constellated upon it.

I will walk home alone with the deep alone,
a disciple of shadows, in praise of the mysteries.

*

—first appeared in *The New Republic*

Song

This is a song for the speechless,
the dumb, the mute and the motley,
the unmourned! This is a song for every
pig that was too thin to be slaughtered
last night, but was slaughtered
anyway, every worm that was hooked
on a hook that it didn't expect,
every chair in New York City that has
no arms or legs, and can't speak English,
every sofa that has ever been torn
apart by the children or the dog
and earmarked for the dump, every sheet
that was lost in the laundry, every
car that has been stripped down and
abandoned, too poor to be towed away,
too weak and humble to protest.
Listen, this song is for you even if
you can't listen to it, or join in;

even if you don't have lungs, even
if you don't know what a song is,
or want to know. This song is for
everyone who is not listening tonight
and refuses to sing. Not singing
is also an act of devotion; those
who have no voices have one tongue.

*

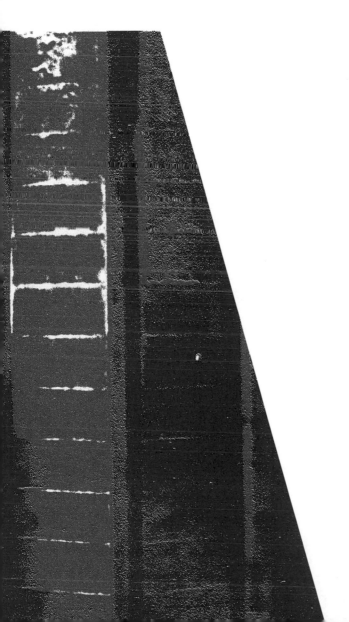

Ocean of Grass

The ground was holy, but the wind was harsh
and unbroken prairie stretched for hundreds of
   miles
so that all she could see was an ocean of grass.

Some days she got so lonely she went outside
and nestled among the sheep, for company.
The ground was holy, but the wind was harsh

and prairie fires swept across the plains,
lighting up the country like a vast tinderbox
until all she could see was an ocean of flames.

She went three years without viewing a tree.
When her husband finally took her on a timber
   run
she called the ground holy and the wind harsh
and got down on her knees and wept
   inconsolably,
and lived in a sod hut for thirty more years
until the world dissolved in an ocean of grass.

Think of her sometimes when you pace the earth,
our mother, where she was laid to rest.
The ground was holy, but the wind was harsh
for those who drowned in an ocean of grass.

The Burning of the Midnight Lamp

Listening to *Purple Haze* and *The Wind
    Cries Mary*,
Let Me Stand Next to Your Fire and *Manic
    Depression*,

I am drifting undersea toward strobe lights
and feedback, the dreamy, acoustic waves of
    1969.

Remember how you explained those dirty
    sounds—
the two-note riff banned by the Spanish
    Inquisition,

the hammer-ons and pull-offs, the sharpened
    ninth?
Is it tomorrow or just the end of time?
I've forgotten nothing. Any moment I'll cross
the campus near the dormitory where you've
    moved in
with another man; I'll pause under the window
    trembling

with volume—a betrayer betrayed and turning
   back

to the raw, metallic, bristling taste of wind.
The morning is dead and the day is too

There's nothing left here to lead me, but the
   velvet moon
(you always like the wah-wah pedal on that
   song).
...
Someone is playing *Voodoo Child* and *House
   Burning Down*,
checking the chord progression in *Spanish Castle
   Magic*

and the octaves in *Third Stone from the Sun*.
Another is blasting *Crosstown Traffic* from a
   lounge

where darkness branches into maroon rivers
and cigarette butts flare into the stars.

No more parties with our friends eating seeds
and lacing punch, smoking joints in dim room

where you go on talking about sinister bent
   strings
and dive-bombing sounds, the devil invoked

in the interval of a tritone or flattened fifth.
No more waiting for you to return to me.
(*that forgotten earring lying on the floor*)
through a downpour of left-handed notes.

But sometimes when I close my eyes
I see your body fading back into shadows.
...
As a child, Jimi Hendrix watched his soul floating
away from his torso, looking down at himself

from a different realm. He was awake but
   slipping
mindlessly through another dimension, the astral
   plane.
That's how you felt about LSD and STP,
Those ten milligram doses of sublime.

We were looking for fire escapes: ladders
and watchtowers spiraling up from the ground.

But that year as I smoldered within my body
and you tripped through the acid nights

Orpheus stomped microphones and humped
   speakers,

smashing amplifiers on stage after stage
as though he could whammy the Underworld
into submission and subdue the Furies

while darkness vibrated around him
and electric guitars exploded in flames.

from **eulogy of jimi christ**

"look at the sky

turn a hell fire red lawd
somebodies house is burnin down down down

"look at the sky turn a hell fire red lawd
somebodies house is burnin down down down
  down...."

—*jimi hendrix*

I.

burn it down

you burned it all the way down jimi

made us burn
in the flame
that became yo sound jimi

grabbed ol legba
by his neck
made him
show you yo respect

hoochieman
coochie man
stranglin him
hoochie coochie hoodooman
wrangled him voodoo chile

made
his
steel
strings sing
ache
bend
break

sin
capitulate
give in
to the will
of yo beautifully
blessed fingers

bewitchinly
bleedin

bittersweet
south paw
serendipitous
sighs

and strained
stratacaster tears

soothin burnin
twistin turnin
into steam
as they fell

no

careened
toward all hellbound souls

only to
roll

back into yo
gypsied eyes
to fornicate
copulate
be sodomized
by penetration beautiful
of sweatband born acid rain

II.

a purple haze runnin through
yo brain drained into the veins

of daytrippers turned acid angel
by yo gift of little wings

which with the aid
of yo mary cryin winds soared
not merely above
around and through
crosstown traffic

but along/well beyond
watchtowers to realm
where gods made love
to little miss strange
foxy ladies in little red houses
over yonder

and on rainy days
would sit back
shoot craps
with laughin sams dice
while boastin bout who had
the most experience

III.

how that musebruise
of yo sadomasochistic bluesoozed
through floors and l.s.d. doors

left psychedelic relics wrecked
on phosphorescent shores

talkin bout that night
you got right
at yo height

rocked woodstock
played yo remade
american anthem...

*

Regie Gibson

marvin bell

track 8

To Dorothy

You are not beautiful, exactly.
You are beautiful, inexactly.
You let a weed grow by the mulberry
and a mulberry grow by the house.
So close, in the personal quiet
of a windy night, it brushes the wall
and sweeps away the day till we sleep.

A child said it, and it seemed true:
"Things that are lost are all equal."
But it isn't true. If I lost you,
the air wouldn't move, nor the tree grow.
Someone would pull the weed, my flower.
The quiet wouldn't be yours. If I lost you,
I'd have to ask the grass to let me sleep.

To No One in Particular

Whether you sing or scream,
the process is the same.
You start, inside yourself,
a small explosion, the difference
being that in the scream
the throat is squeezed so that
the back of the tongue
can taste the brain's fear.
Also, spittle and phlegm
are components of the instrument.
I guess it would be possible
to take someone by the throat
and give him a good beating.
All the while, though, some fool
would be writing down the notes
of the victim, underscoring
this phrase, lightening this one,
adding a grace note and a trill

and instructions in one of those languages
revered for its vowels.
But all the time, it's consonants
coming from the throat.
Here's the one you were throttling,
still gaggin out the guttural ch—-
the throat clearing, Yiddish ch—-
and other consonants spurned by
opera singers and English teachers.
He won't bother you again.
He'll scrape home to take it out
on his wife, more bestial consonants
rising in pitch until spent.
Then he'll lock a leg over her
and snore, and all the time
he hasn't said a word we can repeat.
Even though we all speak his language.
Even though the toast in our throats
in the morning has a word for us—
not at all like bread in rain,

but something grittier in something
thicker, going through what we are.
Even though we snort and sniffle,
cough, hiccup, cry and come
and laugh until our stomachs turn.
Who will write down this language?
Who will do the work necessary?
Who will gag on a chickenbone
for observation? Who will breathe perfectly
under water? Whose slow murder
will disprove for all the time
an alphabet meant to make sense?
Listen! I speak to you in one tongue,
but every moment that ever mattered to me
occurred in another language.
Starting with my first word.
To no one in particular.

Marvin Bell

Anodyne

I love how it swells
into a temple where it is
held prisoner, where the god
of blame resides. I love
slopes & peaks, the secret
paths that make me selfish.
I love my crooked feet
shaped by vanity & work
shoes made to outlast
Belief. The hardness
coupling milk it can't
fashion. I love the lips,
salt & honeycomb on the tongue.
The hair holding off rain
& snow. The white moons
on my fingernails. I love
how everything begs
blood into song & prayer
inside an egg. A ghost
hums through my bones
like Pan's midnight flute
shaping internal laws
beside a troubled river.
I love this body
made to weather the storm

in the brain, raised
out of the deep smell
of fish & water hyacinth,
out of rapture & the first
regret. I love my big hands.
I love it clear down to the soft
quick motor of each breath,
the liver's ten kinds of desire
& the kidney's lust for sugar.
This skin, this sac of dung
& joy, this spleen floating
like a compass needle inside
nighttime, always divining
West Africa's dusty horizon.
I love the birthmark
posed like a fighting cock
on my shoulder blade.
I love this body, this
solo & ragtime jubilee
behind the left nipple,
because I know I was born
to wear out at least
one hundred angels.

*

Blue Light Lounge Sutra for the Performance Poets at Harold Park Hotel

the need gotta be
so deep words can't
answer questions
all night long notes
stumble off the tongue
& color the air indigo
so deep fragments of gut
& flesh cling to the song
you gotta get into it
so deep salt crystallizes on eyelashes
the need gotta be
so deep you can vomit up ghosts
& not feel broken
till you are no more
than a half ounce of gold
in painful brightness
you gotta get into it
blow that saxophone
so deep all the sex & dope in this world
can't erase your need
to howl against the sky
the need gotta be
so deep you can't

just wiggle your hips
& rise up out of it
chaos in the cosmos
modern man in the pepperpot
you gotta get hooked
into every hungry groove
so deep the bomb locked
in rust opens like a fist
into it so deep
rhythm is pre-memory
the need gotta be basic
animal need to see
& know the terror
we are made of honey
cause if you wanna dance
this boogie be ready
to let the devil use your head
for a drum.

*

hip hop

* part 2

(tracks 9–13)

While the image of the Beats as scruffy, drug-taking, writing "angel headed hipsters," started a cult following, they were quickly dismissed by the publishing world or co-opted into the universities. More importantly, however, their ideology gave swift passage for the hippies. By the time the Beats were being recognized for their literary merits, Ken Kesey had traveled the country with his acid pilgrimage, hippies were beginning to sprout, and the Beatles had trudged to the American side of the ocean. With Vietnam at the forefront, social art had become the only important art form. Multiculturalism, feminism, a new historianism…these were the new buzzwords of the literary landscape. And all the while, very quietly, confessional poetry with Robert Lowell, Sylvia Plath, and Anne Sexton leading the way, had slipped into the popular anthologies. More than ever, a commingling of poetics was crossing several different boundaries. And whether consciously driving in this direction or not, by the late '70s and early '80s, poetry had dried itself up altogether in many mediums. However, in the wake of these occurrences, a small revolution began among the black community that would later overshadow many of these smaller aesthetic quibblings.

Hip hop, although undefined at this point, had begun to enter the urban environments by the late '60s with the poetry of The Last Poets who adapted many of the oral attempts of the Beats and went well beyond them in terms of style. By 1972, the idea of rapping was seeded. Aesthetically, rap was most influenced by Jamaican DJ music. The Jamaican DJs like U-Roy were really the first rappers.

Jamaican "sound systems" starting from the early '70s consisted of mobile DJs spinning dub versions of popular rhythm tracks with MCs (half singer/half rappers) "chatting" over them. There weren't bands in these situations, just an MC with a microphone and someone spinning the records. In fact, Kool Herc, the unofficial first rapper, was Jamaican, and that was the concept he was trying to put over. Instead of using popular Jamaican rhythms, the early rappers were using popular rhythm tracks from American R&B, disco, and funk groups like Chic ("Good Times") and rapping over them. Rap, as such, was picking up and expanding the qualities of oral performance.

The first rappers included Grand Master Flash and the Furious Five, Melle Mel, Sugar Hill Gang, Afrika Bambaata, and others. At the beginning, they referred to themselves as MCs, and while they might not have associated themselves as spoken word artists, the link to them has certainly grown dramatically. Later, there were MCs who had a more poetic background and had studied the works of Langston Hughes, Nikki Giovanni, Gil Scott-Heron and others, but initially, rap had more to do with the street and talking hype than it did with poetry. While the term "hip hop" didn't crop up until sometime after the art form started to develop, it's a word that you can hear in the Sugar Hill Gang's "Rappers Delight," just as BeBop was something you might hear Dizzy Gillespie scat. Then it just became the name for the genre. But this was definitely a revolution, a new culture of art, helping create and develop spoken word largely among the black community at first.

regie gibson

funknawlegy
(a never ending quest)

"is there funk after death?   is seven up?"
                              —parliament

!

funk

be the baby
of james browns loins
wet nursin corn liquor
from george clintons nipple

a moon lipped lover
with moon shinin tongue
translatin the song
of footsteps heard sneakin
out back doors

funk

be a dance floor
filled with magenta faith
ridin ragin reefer smoke
into veins of a
brand new fix

funk

be the resurrected
scream of sunbeams
stumblin on junkies
noddin silently towards death

funk

be the honey suckle breath
of women made of star shit
comin in they lovers mouths
like holocausts of screams and laughter
opalescent banshees   shrouded in clouds
devourin the snaggle toothed smile of night

!!

funk

be michael jacksons robot
turned funkadelic poplock

an epiphany brought by a thumb
thumpin strings of a fretless bass
buildin black sound thick enough to
stand on

so intangible
you cant put your hands on

funk

be a thousand fists risin
in rebellion and revolution
grabbin bits of sky
tryin to weave new solutions

funk

be rural blues
learnin to pimp in urban shoes
after payin city dues

warnin ! warnin !

good funk been known
to cause young girls
to find out theys gots hips to use

and this could turn
them into night mamas   **(uuhh)**
with thighs   **(uuhh)**
capable of punkin men   **(good gawd)**
into pieces of dead religion

funk

be a head full of snappy naps
and cokabugs picked out
leanin like a halo
gleamin with the power
of afro sheen and disco baptism

funk

be the gisem of a whisper
soothin as sage smoke
opiatin yo head in
twelve gauge thoughts

funk

be livin and dyin

be sighin and cryin

funk

be a sister swearin she gots
"good hair"

but the kitchen
don caught her ass lyin

funk

be a brand new hog
rollin in pretentious redness
down the center of
rainslicked ghetto streets

cuttin up asphalt
with all the tenacity
of a new car payment
through a welfare check

funk

be the groovy groove
of a lovers hand dippin
down to drown yo groin
in a project stairwell echoin the smelly serenade
of piss stains framed on gray walls like abstract
   hieroglyphs

funk

be somethin you got to go back
and get cuz

to dig what funk is
you gots to cop
what funk was

!!!

funk

was yo teeth stained green and red
from a combination of sour apple
and wala-melon nialters
and chic-o-stick breath
stankin to the tune of pop-rock candy

funk

by definition was not
jim nor dandy
amos nor andy
or barry man u low singing mandy

funk

was that three-quarter inch of vaseline
black southern mamas rubbed on black
childrens faces
on blustery winter mornins
fo we went off to school

cuz they
mississippi
alabama
tennessee
louisiana
georgia
arkansas
north
south cakalakee

common sense
told them that theoretically speakin
northern wind should whip round brown chillun
   faster
if they be properly lubricated

and funk was that feelin
of relief we felt upon
arrivin at school and diggin
how we was just one of a tiny   shiny
group of greasy faced youngsters

whose black southern mamas
was obviously matriculated
from the same school of thought

funk

was communion

funk

said come you on

funk

looked at you
like that last swig of red kool-aid
or piece of sweet potato pie
at a black family reunion

funk

was and is a sunday mornin
church girl singin first alto
in the choir
tryin to forget
all the sins she committed
on that saturday night funk found her

and funk was and is that brother
sittin way in the back
three hallelujahs
and a praise gawd
from the right who cant wait
til church is over so he can remind her

funk

be a **funkee** poet
knittin a **funkee** net
of **funkee** words

realizin the **funkee** futility
of tryin to capture **funk** in a poem

*hip hop hop Poetry

(by Jerry Quickley)

you want me to clown myself
and collapse the distance between poetry and hip hop
'what the heck' ain't no substitution for rhyme absolutions
like Popeye with spinach hip hop's my constitution
who you think you foolin' like you don't understand this
cause I'm the son of Run and you the son of Elvis

First off, hip hop is poetry. All of it. Not all of it is good poetry. But it's all poetry. The world is filled with mediocre and bad poetry. Much of it is found in rap, college programs (students and instructors), the academy, coffeehouses, adverts, and everywhere else it's being produced. Hip hop embodies a form of poetry just like sonnets, villanelles, litanies, renga, and other forms. Hip hop incorporates many of the technical devices of other forms, including slant rhymes, enjambment, A-B rhyme schemes, and other techniques, usually parsed in sixteen-bar stanzas, and generally followed by four-to-eight-bar hooks. In this sense, hip hop is a form. Nothing more.

In the broadest strokes, rap began with a confluence of events in New York City during the mid-'70s. The context of the New York music scene in that period was overwhelmingly disco, older R&B and funk bands, punk, and increasingly tired mainstream rock. While there were bright moments to be found in all those forms, not one of them succeeded in truly connecting with and embracing black youth.

It's not so much that the record industry was ignoring kids in New York; they were ignoring black kids and Latino kids from poor neighborhoods. The attitude was largely: who gives a shit what the kids in the ghettos like or what they listen to? This created a massive void. Rap provided the disenfranchised youth of New York self-valorization and a new secret language that was created by cracking open English and stuffing it with new meaning.

Fast forward to the present. Rap has grown from a few thousand kids running around the streets of New York to a global movement. In these terms, hip hop is perhaps the most revolutionary art movement to come along in one hundred years. But just as any revolution provides positive movement, some steps backward occur.

Hip hop is filled with all the contradictions, problems, and challenges that any cultural and political movement with hundreds of millions of participants inevitably possesses. The problem is not the hip hop stars of the moment. The problem is not Jay-Z. The problem is that the gatekeepers, massively consolidated radio conglomerates, music promoters, and label executives that effectively control what is released put the vast majority of their efforts only behind Jay-Z and Nelly and the like. There needs to be broader support by the labels and media outlets for the diversity of voices in hip hop, and not just for P. Diddy and Ja Rule. The distortion and over-amplification of a very narrow section of hip hop is messing up the program. Media execs all too often define themselves with safe, easy choices. Homogenization is much easier and safer for radio stations and labels than innovation and the massive risks of capital that are part of it. The real problem of hip hop comes with whom P. Diddy and Jay-Z and DMX and Eminem have sided, not with the work they do. At critical moments, they have cast their lot with the wealthy instead of the have-nots. Who you choose to cast your lot with defines the mark you leave on the world. The difference between Boots Riley and Master P is defined by a great deal more than record sales.

But it's also important that true hip hop and its mission be kept in perspective. Ninety-nine percent of hip hop sold is from only 1 or 2 percent of hip hop artists who have deals at major

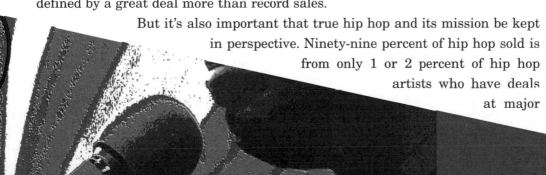

labels and the global distribution that comes with it. Underground hip hop represents the vast majority that is produced in the United States and around the world. Underground hip hop remains "CNN for black people." Artists like the Mountain Brothers, Mike Ladd, People Under the Stairs, Bambu, Project Blowed, Lone Catalyst, Planet Asia, 2Mex, BusDriva, Choclair, Les Princes Des Villes, Aztlan Underground, Wise Guy Gastone, Drez, Aceyalone, Dead Prez, and The Coup represent some of the most diverse and consistently progressive voices coming out of the underground scene. And there are many who came out of the underground that have moved to big labels (Ozo, Dilated, The Roots, Black Eyed Peas, MadLib, Mystic, Blackalicious, MOS Def, Company Flow, and lots more) and are still laying it down and representing with beats, party tracks, and progressive vibe. But most of these artists are not given nearly the support their talent warrants, regardless of the content.

Hip hop, where it has been and where it is going, has very strong connections to the world of performance poetry and slam. The early history of hip hop provides a (somewhat spooky) ghost image that much of performance poetry is following to a degree. Some of that bodes well, and the rest…well, let's just say keep your hands on your wallets and try not to get fatal lockjaw from the near-certain soon-to-materialize parade of clowns who'll be doing their best to induce chronic TMJ—a condition to the jaw—to lovers of the word.

Hip hop is a lifestyle and worldview much more than it is a set of discs or clothes. It's no surprise then that as more poets grew up in the hip hop generation and have come into the world of slam poetry, that we see hip hop's innovative aesthetic interconnect and create new forms. While there has been evidence of this as far back as Paul Beatty in 1990, there was a seismic shift that took place at the National Poetry Slam in Portland, Oregon, in 1996. Three of the four members of Team Nuyorican were young black artists, heavily grounded in the work of their peers in hip hop and for whom hip hop culture was strongly interwoven in their work. Even the one Asian American member (Beau Sia) of that year's Nuyorican team seemed to have his work rooted in a kind of fearless punk rock/hip hop self-consciousness. MuMs tha' Schema, Jessica Care Moore, and most notably Saul Williams arrived on the national slam stage with a sonic boom. Saul in particular brought the full hip hop style, using human beat box sounds, simulating and miming DJ techniques, and weaving hardware verbiage and rhyme schemes into poems that pondered the irony of wanting to overcome a painful history (personal and political) with not having the strength to bear up under the weight of that history and face it before moving on.

The work that Saul and the rest of 1996's Nuyorican team did that year had been going on for some time already within the work of many young black poets, but had not previously been given the broad recognition and appreciation it received at the National Poetry Slam that year. This was largely due to the Paul Devlin–lensed documentary *SlamNation* that was filmed in Portland. Paul's documentary gave the Nuyoricans (and the rest of slam) a national—and to some degree an international—platform for their work to be seen. And one of the things the world saw was what happens when the young, gifted, and black allow themselves to channel poetry and the sum of their experiences as members of the hip hop generation. When you speak to people who have seen *SlamNation*, particularly those outside the world of poetry, what they refer to over and over again is Saul Williams' performance in that year's finals. It very much felt, and continues to feel, like the early years of hip hop. It was obvious that the world was at the beginning of an exciting and fledgling style that had the possibility to reconfigure the ways in which Spoken Word resonated and connected with people. (Much as slam did and continues to do.)

To actually represent hip hop flavor and styles within poetry, you must be able to represent, or rap, straight hip hop. If you effectively manifest hip hop poetry styles, it means that you have the ability to use both straight up hip hop and straight up poetry (free verse, haiku, sonnets, whatever). Being a poet using hip hop styles does not mean that you throw in some timely ghetto colloquialism and vaguely clever but ultimately overtly self-conscious end rhymes. It means that you can choose to bend styles to your will both within your written

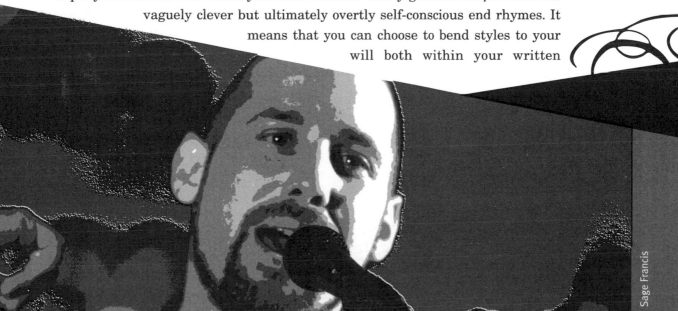

Sage Francis

work and within your performances, all the while keeping your uniqueness and tone intact. There are artists who claim to represent hip hop poetry, and if they were ever caught in a cipher (a group of MCs flowing verse) they would be like the proverbial deer caught in a beat box's headlights.

Over the years, there have been many poets who slam or have slammed that can and do fully represent hip hop poetry styles. Some of these artists include BessKepp from Los Angeles; Piece from Seattle; Sage Francis from Providence; Omalara from San Francisco; Seed from Atlanta; Danny Hoch from New York; Bryonn Bain from New York; Boogie Man from Cleveland; Sarah Jones from New York; DJ Renegade from Washington, D.C.; Rich Medina from Philadelphia; Dennis Kim and Tara Betts from Chicago; and yes, yours truly from New York but currently chilling in the hills of Hollywood.

Just as in the world of hip hop, there will be many periods of styles within slam and performance poetry. Some of them will be truly plangent and innovative. Others would have been better left hidden in a journal. The links between slam and much of hip hop should be obvious, particularly on the business end of art. There is a developing shift within slam from art to commerce. That same shift happened long ago within hip hop. The material Wu did with C.R.E.A.M. was a groundbreaking artistic recognition of the must-get-paid-at-all-costs aesthetic that had long been part of the black community (though at wildly intermittent volumes). As strong as that track is, it also effectively synthesized the greatest conflicts in the commerce of hip hop: "I'm broke. I ain't got shit. I'm tired of tryin' to make a dollar outta fifteen cents. I just want to get paid." That attitude reflects the exhaustion and pessimism that runs through many black communities: "I'm not trying to change the world. I'm just trying to get a time share in Maui." I don't agree with that sentiment, but I can understand where it comes from. Similarly, poets are by and large broke. There is a sense of exhaustion and frustration among many poets that mirrors the sentiments of some black communities. Poverty is violent. It produces all kinds of dysfunction. We see this in the poetry world. Who the emerging band of "professional poets" choose to cast their lot with is not yet definitive. Let's hope we're more original than just wanting the money so we can call our publicists and have them book us on MTV's next season of *Cribs*.

*hear...
track 10

Hip Hop Hollas

A scholar recently asked me about
the relevance of hip hop
I didn't know what to say to him
All I could say was that I remember field hollers
before the preachers got a hold a them

naught's a naught, and five's a figger
all for the white man none for the nigger

brothers is like mine workers, in back rooms
and studios
be massaging the SP 1200's
searchlighting veins of gold
and there be like Stetasonic drumming in my
    ears
Forever my funk flavor Jumbalaya stew
and there be mad endorphine flight/fight rushes
as twelve shell toes leap towards Hollis gat
    bushes

hoe we workin' in high cotton sun
hoe we sweatin' for the devils fun

and there be moments like this
custom coach with 12 niggers on their first tour
gliding at 70 across the desert floor
and there be 12 faces pasted to the windows
Instead a arguing about watching how the money
    goes
they be checking out the blooms of desert rose
and Arizona lightning smells of ozone
and sudden rain washes rocks that dwelled in the
    sea
and there's only the sounds of the engines rotary,
the bright cords of lightning
as heaven manifests subwoofers
ain't all that make the shit mad exciting
it's the snap crackle pop of Tupac
pushed out of Bose cubes

pressing his heart into this moment
and this scene is music
and this moment is an organ
and somewhere there is a
custom coach with 12 niggers on their first tour

fields heavy we waitin' for harvest moon
the chilrens feet never seen no shoes

and there be moments like this
four girlfriends driving out of the hood
going to a party in the oranges
this is the first time the youngest has been alone
in a car with her friends
they zoom across the GW
canopy of steel beams
paints the hoop de in fast blurs of shade and sun
and tires roar from the grates
and up front there's the sound of
bracelets and nails on the dashboard
and there is laughter and
there are no box cutters or police
and L'il Kim jumps through the speakers
and the youngest girl pushes herself
deep into the rear seat
as straining speakers conjure halos
she watches the world sway past
the tiny rear window
and this fat bass line will forever mark this
    turning point
and she has never felt so free
and she has never felt so strong and so loved
these are her niggers
and somewhere a young woman is going
on her first ride with her crew

the mule is down done wore hisself out
gots to pick eight more rows 'fore I give out

and there be moments like this
Nebraska farm boy sitting
on the edge of a quarry pit
all his crystal powder gone
he wonders about gravity
he wonders about his family
his sister writes to him from
a small town in the north
tells him of jesus and fewer black eyes
how he should visit in the summer time
because her boyfriend should be out of rehab
and how the yellin' ain't so bad
his pops tells him next year things will be
    different
and he wonders if he will ever escape next year
    country
and he feels weak inside his strong body
and gravity is making moves
and Jay-Z's Hard Knocks crow from the cab of his
    pick up
and for a few minutes he's lost in it
tales of a life closer than you think
close to the bone it unfurls like his own
runs to a neighboring corn field
he splits stars with his scream
he stands breathless in headlight beams
he smiles and he's high as a kite
and he knows that moonlight and beats have
    saved his life
and somewhere a farm boy
sits on the edge of a quarry

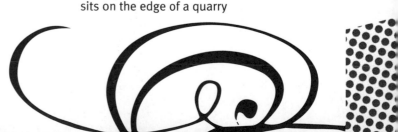

Swing that hook, split and pile tha cane
five cent a day, you ain't gettin' no train

and there be moments like this
with family and friends in the front room
a woman washes dishes at the sink
a mother with missing heart
buried earlier that same day
in the same casket with her young son
and across from their house
a yard party has broken out
and in this moment
her first moments alone
her chest is imploding
failure and loss have arrived
and they will stay for a very long time
and she didn't know hearts could break this hard
or what black magic makes her still draw breath
and in this moment
her first moments alone
De La Soul trickles in the window
and she begins to cry
as the brothers from the east
preach about how the Stakes is High
and somewhere there is an empty mother
washing dishes in a sink by a window

White folks and nigger in da great court house
like a cat down the celler with a no-hole mouse

chorus' been around the world and back again
extracting pain from songs of black skins
sip and sample our shit and sell it back again
cause niggers is caught up in dreams of mackin'
overseers lips was smackin'
as he went out back again
terror has new names and darker faces
cause now niggers is runnin' that shit back again
he crushes her spirit cause it makes him feel like
     Sampson
he don't know the price of the ransom
and doesn't recognize slippery slopes
or the sound of hope dipping out through the
     transom
swollen knuckles drift toward hip hop radio soon
as you hear it pump up the volume
pump that beat
pump that beat
pump that beat
and that's the fucking relevance
of hip hop

*

48 Hours After You Left

The telephone
   has put on a bathrobe,
   complaining that my constant staring
   makes it feel naked,
   And I find myself out in the street
   interrogating raindrops
   as to your whereabouts.
   This one particular raindrop
   keeps being very evasive
   answering in metaphors,
   (I may have to get rough).
   Happiness stumbles along
   smelling of Mad Dog
   and mumbo sauce,
   wearing cheap sneakers

with holes the size
of a headache
and a shirt that reads
like a menu of stains.
I've begun bottling my tears,
to serve as holy water,
and all the vowels
of my vocabulary
are now lookouts
on my windowsill,
waiting to trumpet
your return.

tara betts

Rock'n'Roll Be a Black Woman

Rock'n'Roll be a Black Woman
Where you thank they got the name from?
Black Magic Woman
Brown Sugar
Copper strings stretched on guitar necks
Tan skirts taut on the mouths of drums
Rock'n'Roll be a Black Woman
Plucking as firmly as
Mashing of frets like delicate testicles
jangling under the discord of a well-pedicured foot

Rock'n'Roll be a Black Woman
Eminent as comet tail juice announcing
An ebony-tinged star's exit
Rock'n'Roll be a Black Woman
Furiously embossing the stamp of her man's ass
    into the mattress

Primacy screaming in breasts that fed you
After tired sweat wriggled between them
She be tainted with funk
Permeatin her like chittlin buckets in kitchen sinks

Rock'n'Roll be a Black Woman
Rock'n'Roll be her blood drippin from
twin lips of a crescent moon
Rock'n'Roll be her kissin Papa Legba at
midnight crossroads
Rock'n'Roll be her standin next to the mountain
that she mashes into pebbles with the edge
of her hand
Rock'n'Roll be her creepin
while you sleepin
through yo veins like Mississippi River mud

Rock'n'Roll be a Black Woman
Workin, jerkin
Grindin, windin
Screamin, dreamin
Moanin, groanin
The sounds on loan and
You wonder where where where
Did some white boy get the name for them
    blues?
Maybe he was thinkin of some baby-makin hips
    to abuse 'cuz
Rock'n'Roll be a Black Woman

A Mixed Message

What makes me so damn tragic?
    not a fragmented exotic myster
    jezebel born from the blood of rape
    nor child of the so-called integration
    experiment
I heard folks tell my momma
    How can parents put children through that
    It makes life so much harder,
I have seen my mind
    build bridges within blood
    my biology connects with ovaries & melanin
    with no capital to spare
I explode from Nella Larsen novels
    yet somehow, I am Invisible Woman
    descendant of Invisible Man
    niece of an Ex-Colored Man
I balance proud weight & independent
    discipline
    on scales of identity
    swinging precarious images of Pinky & Pecola
    Decades before my birth

when certificates denied
    evident possibility
    plain as brown freckles
    across my face
    when some enjoyed the milk
    but avoided sunlight honey
    so no secrets would break
    into shards of life on racial concrete
    where I stand whole/deconstructing
    past nicknames
    like zebra, mutt or half-n-half
    while remembering my father
    held me through 11-year-old
    tears calling me by name
    calling me beautiful

Now, some say
    must be Black
    could be white
    maybe she's pinay
    Add Mexican to the list
    Puerto Rican
    tan white girl
    Are you from the South?
    Or the best one yet
    Are you Egyptian?
    At least when I wandered
    a continent where textbooks concealed
    land anchoring the Sphinx

I rekindle links as I touch
    brown hands with palms
    the same shade as mine
    I find myself within
    amalgamation improvisation
    within Black
    contradicting the bubbling brew of
    unidentifiable, indecipherable
    ethnic glamour girls
    What was she anyway?
No Concubine mistress
    nor color caste breeding
    rippin paper bag tests into confetti
    Ready to dissolve with steam rising
    from a glass of other

I defy categories
    fill in all the gaps
    where miscegenation laws
    blotted my birth
My voice smatters blood in the face
    of Aryan Nations
    I am what they feared
    Never passed in the world
    but passed salves over broken flesh
    reclaiming nationhood I lost generations ago
    retracing veins from history's corpse
    resounding with speech
    extending beyond
    now

*

Celena Glenn

celena glenn

hear...

track 11

The Hand Has Turned

the hand has turned
and I will no longer sit
behind a locked bathroom door
with faucet racing to quiet the grunts of my fury

in the streets I must mourn
my disgust with this lost, forgotten marble

find me sharing sips with winos
and massaging whores
for they have not turned their face
to the fact that this universe
is tired of filtering our carbon

we the people
are killing softly the light of the moon
with our street lamps and radiation

we pretend we spin the earth on our tongues
and can count all the stars before we fall

only the wind will continue to blow
even if we cease to follow

this land does not need our filth
this electron does not need negativity
for its opposite is neutral
and neutral is positive when persuaded

I persuade the sleeping to rise
and live life as the sun
and the dead to, as dust

I persuade this life to live in me
so that I can one day carry this universe
like a metrocard to a new found world

*

URBANA — "I NAIL MY PALMS" TRACK #7

We try to spin the earth on our tongue
And count the stars before they fall
Only the wind will continue to blow
Even if we don't follow

BEAT STOPS

We try to spin the earth on our tongue
And count the stars before they fall
Only the wind will continue to blow
Even if we don't follow

I nail my palms
With my pen
To my desk
And confess all of my committed sins
I forgive my self and move forward

Like the book of psalms
I read like parables
Stories of the weight of the world
Endured in both triumph and defeat
I lay my soul at your feet
and place my heart on the line
hoping that blind eyes will see

We try to spin the earth on our tongue
And count the stars before they fall
Only the wind will continue to blow
Even if we don't follow

BASS ONE TIME
"THEN BELIEVE IN ME." W/ BASS HARMONY

I have returned
And will continue
For this existence is merely a venue
That will succeed or decease
Too close to its beginning
Depending on the loyalty of its consumers
Wool coats who where false convictions
Who quickly stray from the flock
Of conscious conspirators
Collaborating to reclaim
Once conquered dynasties
Deities living in the dark
Not following the light
But the light from within
Tempted not to follow the vessel
But paralleling with its contents
I am that prophecy

NO BASS

I am inspiration and torment experienced and foreseen
I nail my heart
With my pen to my desk and I bleed

ECHO WORDS

I am inspiration and torment experienced and foreseen
I nail my heart
With my pen to my desk and I bleed

BASS BACK WITH WORDS

Your fears are my own

Only refuge can not house my thoughts
I speak with the intent to penetrate
Veiled luminosity's
In which you are lost
Looking for a way out
Or simply following the wrong flock

I need you to believe in not me
But my words
Help me to carry the weight
When the winds of the world
Blow briskly
With an unfathomable fiction
Not like the parables in my psalms

BASS BACK TO NOTES

— GEORGE OUT!

We try to spin the earth on our tongue
And count the stars before they fall
Only the wind will continue to blow
Even if we don't follow

BEAT OUT

Thoughts only exist
When they are listened to
So give me reason
Give me life
I don't want to cry alone at your feet

BEAT OUT

WORDS

I am sinking into torment
Because I see no inspiration
Am I blind
Or is there no light radiating
To keep me in rotation with the sky

← BEAT BACK

I nail my soul
With my pen
to my desk and cry

I nail my soul
With my pen
to my desk and cry

can you hear me

DO NOT WORRY. IT IS NOT YOU! THE JUDGES SUCK. IT'S A POETRY SLAM!

PROTEST DENIED

By Celena Glenn

Kevin Coval

Hear O' Israel

Hear o' Israel
the star belongs to no one
for not David would believe
his child has become Goliath
spitting imperialist warheads
at children holding slingshots

if you are to be perfection
we must teach ourselves
lessons missed assimilating
bacon breakfasts under the Christmas tree
with cleavers cutting bumps off our hooked
    noses
driving roman chariots on the Sabbath
to execute eviction notices in ghettos
we once were wrangled in too.

Israel
you are the messenger
sent to gather ye children
of meta-tongue and supplication

have you lost your way?

hunting salvation like lynch mob
in traife corners of anglo lands
you whore yourself to sleep
in the hands of men who will beat you
after morning coffee.

Israel
you pawn. middle east
western military base.
you are strategic oil insurance
for american mongrels
who cut language from our lips
with english-named conversions
who re-stitched circumcisions
mohels made with television wire
who put bread and prosperity
before our famished mouths
we gnaw the covenant till it breaks
centuries of Rivka's teachings.

at our own funerals
we worship the emperor's idols
like they were our G-d's.

we wonder the diaspora dead.

Israel,
where is Judith to chop off your head?
what have you done with Rabbi Nachman?

can you be chosen alone
in an interconnected universe?

will you open your doors
to all children who cry
silent in bombed nights??

Lebanon and Ramallah, Jerusalem and Chechnya

your daughters wandered forty years
seeking a place to rest their family
praise existence, birth future messiahs
who will bring forth baruch words
in the ears of G-d's millioned mouths

will you listen Israel?

for the messenger calls constant

but before which altar
do you burn incense?

i saw you in South Africa
quiet in the back room
Steve Biko's holy hands
were murdered in.

in Liberia your diamonds drip dead
fingerprints, fund limousines for the Rebbe
to view memorial cheesecake tourist factories
in Tel Aviv city centers wailing at the walls
of consumption.

i can no longer witness thousands of murdered
Palestinian children dragged on the empty box
that stares nightly into my face and say i can't
          see
what you are doing

·i see you Israel

and yes i saw you
in Crown Heights murdered by half brothers
walking on eggshells since destruction of the
          first temple
and yes i think they might come for us again
and yes i imagine Gestapo with new uniforms
Austrian, German, or Confederate
and yes i am scared to wear my yarmulke in
          public
because i don't want numbers burned into my
          skin
or to be asked to show my horns

i am paranoid with historical precedence
but i am not my self
Israel, who are you?
your message is cryptic
and i can't read Hebrew

Shema israel addonai elchainu addonai echad

the lord is one, Israel
so when will you
stop killing yourself?

hear...

track 13

Amethyst Rocks

"what i got
come and get some
(get on up)
hustler of culture"

i stand on the corner of the block slingin'
　　amethyst rocks
drinkin' 40s of Mother Earth's private nectar
　　stock

dodgin' cops
'cause five-O are the 666
and i need a fix of that purple rain
the type of shit that drives membranes insane

oh yes, i'm in the fast lane
snorting...candy yams
that free my body and soul
and send me like Shazam!

"never question
who i am
god knows"

and i know god personally
in fact, he lets me call him me

i be one with rain and stars and things
with dancing feet and watermelon wings
i bring the sunshine and the moon
and the wind blows my tune
...meanwhile
i spoon powdered drum beats into plastic bags
sellin' kilos of kente scag

takin' drags off of collards and cornbread
free-basing through saxophones and flutes like
　　mad

the high notes make me space float
i be exhalin' in rings that circle Saturn
leavin' stains in my veins in astrological patterns

yeah, i'm sirius B
Dogon' niggas plotted shit, lovely
but the Feds are also plottin' me
they're tryin' to imprison my astrology
to put my stars behind bars
my stars in stripes
using blood splattered banners
as nationalist kites
but i control the wind
that's why they call it the hawk
i am horus
son of isis
son of osiris
worshipped as jesus
resurrected like lazarus
but you can call me lazzie
lazy
yeah, i'm lazy
cause i'd rather sit and build
than work and plow a field
worshipping a daily yield of cash green crops

your evolution stopped
with the evolution of your technology
a society of automatic tellers
and money machines
nigga what?

my culture is lima beans
and tambourines
dreams manifest
dreams real
not consistent with rational
I dance fɔ· nɔ· ·eaʃɔn
for reasons you can't dance
caught in the inactiveness of intellectualized
    circumstance
you can't learn my steps until you unlearn my
    thoughts
spirit soul can't be store bought

fuck thought
it leads to naught
simply stated it leads to you
tryin' to figure me out

your intellect is disfiguring soul
your beings not whole
check your flag pole:
stars and stripes
your astrology is imprisoned
by your concept of white
of self
what's your plan of spiritual health?
calling reality unreal
your line of thought is tangled
the star spangled got your soul mangled
your beings angled
forbidding you to be real and feel
you can't find truth with an ax or a drill
in a white house on a hill
or in factories or plants made of steel

s t e a l i n g   m e
was the smartest thing you ever did
too bad you don't teach the truth to your kids
my influence on you is the reflection you see
when you look into your minstrel mirror
and talk about your culture

your existence is that of a schizophrenic vulture
who thinks he has enough life in him
to prey on the dead
not knowing
that the dead ain't dead
and that he ain't got enough spirituality
to know how to pray
yeah, there's no repentance

you're bound to live
an infinite consecutive executive life sentence
so while you're busy serving your time
i'll be in sync with the moon
while you run from the sun
life of the womb
reflected by guns
worshipper of moons
i am the sun
and i am public enemy number one
one one one
one one one
that's seven
and i'll be out on the block

hustlin' culture
slingin' amethyst rocks

Saul Williams

The future of Language

(by Saul Williams)

A Latin transcription of the word person is "being of sound." As human beings, we communicate with each other and the greater universe through sound vibration. It is thus the essence of our collective being. All sounds reverberate with meaning. Every sound vibration has an effect and every sound is connected with every word we speak, and every syllable is connected to its eternal meaning, its eternal reverberation. The original inhabitants of Egypt actually documented the esoteric meaning of each sound vibration. They believed that all consonant sounds communed with energies of a temporal reality, whereas vowel sounds connected with energies of the eternal reality. In their written text, they only wrote consonants, for the eternal reality was too sacred to be transcribed. The ancient Egyptian language, like all other languages of antiquity, was rooted in passion. Yet over time, many cultures have become disconnected from the passionate roots of their own language and thus, perhaps, disconnected from the root of human existence.

In the east, it is widely believed that the word/sound "om" is the seed of the universe and that the seed of all creation can be heard reverberating within all life forms. Practically all religions over time have focused on the power of sound vibration. Whether through the chanting of "om," Buddhist and Hindu chants, Islamic prayers and calls to worship, or reciting "Hail Mary" and the Lord's Prayer, the common thread has been the investment in the belief that change will come about through voicing sacred words aloud. Yet, like the ancient Egyptians, many of these belief systems have also held to the idea that there is a realm of eternal reality

that cannot be put into words. In the words of the eastern mystic Lao Tzu, the Tao that can be told is not the eternal Tao. The name that can be named is not the eternal name. The unnamable is the eternally real. Naming is the origin of all particular things.

Thus, the future of language would involve us getting closer and closer to being able to articulate the unspoken. Consciousness, like technology, evolves over time. In the same way that there are advances made in technology that may take a decade or more before they reach the public, there are also shifts in consciousness that readily become understandable by the masses over time. For example, an idea that perhaps the twelfth Dalai Lama achieved through meditation, however many years ago, may just be reaching the level of common understanding by the average young American today. Ideas and concepts that perhaps our parents could not grasp until mid-life crisis may be now grasped by adolescent teens. And things that once could only be put into words by the most learned philosophers can now be expressed by the average MC (and in my estimation most MCs that I hear are average).

I had the privilege of cowriting a film called *Slam*, the story of a young kid who learns the power of word and uses it to transcend his given reality. In writing this film, I decided to give the main character the last name Joshua, based on the biblical story of Joshua who fought the battle of Jericho by simply marching around the city's walls seven times playing his trumpet; the walls came tumbling down. I figured that if the film was played on seven hundred screens, the walls of Babylon would come tumbling down, mainly because of the spells laced into the poetry of the film. I have often thought of my poetry in terms of it being incantations: spells or prayers to be recited in the darkest caves and the highest mountain tops. In writing, I often feel as if I am deciphering age-old equations and am often as baffled an audience member as any other listener or reader. I have also been in numerous occasions where I have felt that I wrote or recited a situation into existence.

Language usage is a reflection of consciousness; thus, the future of language is co-related to the ever-evolving

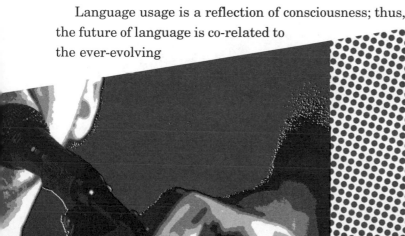

state of human awareness. As we become more aware of our existing reality, it becomes clear that we live with the power of dictating our given situations and thus the power to determine our future. Our present reality is pre-sent, dictated by what we asked for previously. No, I am not saying that everything that happens to us is within our control, but through our perceptions we have the ability to determine much more of our reality than we realize (all puns intended). And what we say (which is clearly a reflection of what and how we think) is of the utmost (uttermost) importance. What we say matters (becomes a solid: flesh).

So then the question becomes, what role does hip hop play in the future of language? Or rather, what role does the future of language play in hip hop? There does seem to have been a lyrical evolution in hip hop. Vivid, descriptive narratives of ghetto life seem to have come at the cost of imaginative or psycho-spiritual exploration. In other words, niggas have come up with amazing ways to talk about the same ol' shit. The problem is, when we recite the same ol' shit into microphones that increase sound vibration, the same ol' shit continues to manifest in our daily lives. But, of course, employing one's imagination is problematic when the aim is to keep it real. In a book called *Illusions* by Richard Bach, the main character finds that when Jesus reportedly said that all one needs is faith the size of a mustard seed to move mountains, he actually only said faith because at the time there wasn't a word for imagination. It is imagination applied to our daily lives and use of language that brings about interesting futures. Hip hop, as is, is mainly concerned with depicting a rough street life devoid of hope, or an upscale designer life devoid of thought, and in so doing dictates its own outcome. If Biggie's album had not been entitled *Ready to Die,* would he still be alive today? Did his vocalized profession dictate his destination? The fact that we were so ready to hear about how he was ready to die increased the sound vibration of his recitation through playing it on a million radios and televisions at a time to the point where it affected our reality and his.

performance art

part 3

(tracks 14–16)

introduction

In the wake of the '60s social consciousness, the development of postmodernism and structuralism had begun. In an attempt to breathe life back into the art, to decenter the social and the individual, postmodern poetry attempted to give meaning to the form rather than the author. With Derrida leading the charge under the guise of Deconstruction, personal viewpoint was interpreted as biased viewpoint, and art was revalued as nothing more than individual quarrels meant to persuade the reader. What a text says, if anything, and how it was important became more important than what it expressed. The form became the art. Objectivity became king. And while this writing might be important for the professional reader, the university professor, the theorist, or graduate students seeking approval from old blue-hairs, this writing was exclusive and open to few. And, more importantly, it was boring.

Perhaps one can go as far back as Vachel Lindsey and his reading of "Congo" at the Dill Pickle Club to see that poetry was being read and performed out loud to some degree at the early part of the century. Again, in 1956, Allen Ginsberg's inspirational and impassioned reading of *Howl* seemed to recognize the need for poets to do more than just read poems at an audience. But both of these examples seem to be driven by personalities who had a flair for the stage. While both powerful figures with an audience, neither poet claimed the importance of creating a show for the audience. Perhaps it was John Giorno who first brought to light the idea of entertainment and poetry going hand in hand:

John Ashbery, who lived in Paris, moved back to New York. And Frank O'Hara gave a poetry reading at some gallery in the seventies on the East Side [New York]. I went with Andy Warhol. It was a hot, June night, really hot, and it was packed, because John was famous at that point, in his little "world." It was packed. There were a hundred and twenty five people, and John and Frank up at the front there, we couldn't hear a word. Andy kept saying over and over again, "It's so boring. It's so boring," and "Why does it have to be so boring?" (*Impure: Reinventing the Word*, Stanton and Tinguely, 2001, p. 69.)

Giorno created "environment" poetry, where the setting of the poetry reading becomes just as important as the reading. He was one of the first of the new wave of performance artists, and possibly the first who consciously combined poetry and performance together. Although he may have been one of the first, the arena of Performance Art was to take off dramatically.

Performance Art

performance Poetry
—The Two Sisters
(by Jean Howard)

When I first arrived in Chicago in 1979, the poetry scene was a quietly humming series of readings, like the Banyan Press series at the Paul Wagoner Gallery, and the Poetry Center readings featuring "top name" poets like Philip Levine and Galway Kinnell. Although the Poetry Center brought in larger audiences, these series tended to bring in the same small pockets of people for audiences—poets, "poets hearing poets."

The local performance art scene, on the other hand, was definitely kicking off. Raw spaces and galleries like Randolph Street Gallery were showcasing weekly groundbreaking performance art featuring abstraction, physicality, visual manipulation, lighting, sound texture, pyrotechnics, and other sensory mechanisms. The experimentation that audiences not only were exposed to, but also participated in, left them charged and returning for more.

It was in this environment that I met neon/metal sculptor Tom Scarff, who was well established in the art community, and who at the time was experimenting with dance and movement. Scarff had been showing his neon in the '60s wrapped within trees, or snaking through sand dunes, and moved his art now into the realm of human relationships. He approached me with the prospect of collaborating on a work called "The Argon," a performance piece incorporating neon, sculpture, costuming, sound, movement, and poetry, presented a matriarchal society existing in a world created by argon (the gas creating yellow neon). This was followed by

"Climax Deluxe," a collaboration with dancer/choreographer Pat Fischer Selby, a video artist, Bob Boldt, a sound artist, Ted Garner, and Tom Scarff, performed at Frumkin Struve Gallery. It was even more experimental, with the complete performance taking place behind a wall while audience members viewed it from their only access, two monitors mounted on the wall. Playing to a packed house, one of the more important spectators was Marc Smith, an emerging poet also seeking alternative ways to express his work.

Nationally, at this time, the work of Chicago-born performance artist Laurie Anderson was making its presence known to mainstream audiences. Karen Finley, another Chicagoan, would gain a certain notoriety, not for smearing chocolate pudding and other substances over/into her body while performing confrontational poetry about the abuse of women, but because the National Endowment of the Arts pulled its funding of her because of that work.

Locally, other venues were opening up to poets. A few bars offered up poetry one night a week, putting poetry into the bar/cabaret scene and allowing more unorthodox and demonstrative poets to step up. The traditional stagnant reading of a poem was no match for the level of audience engagement possible when poetry was presented as a physical/full sensory experience. For a few experimenting poets, like myself, there was no turning back.

One of the earliest, most primitive nightspots opened to experimenting performance poets was the Get Me High Lounge located in a north side, blue collar Chicago neighborhood. This small, dark, graffiti-walled bar offered a stage with the bathroom located in back, so patrons had to walk on stage during performances to gain access to it. Marc Smith had secured Monday nights, a traditionally dead night at the bar, to showcase the handful of poets exploring performance art. Local neighborhood patrons trying to watch a Cubs

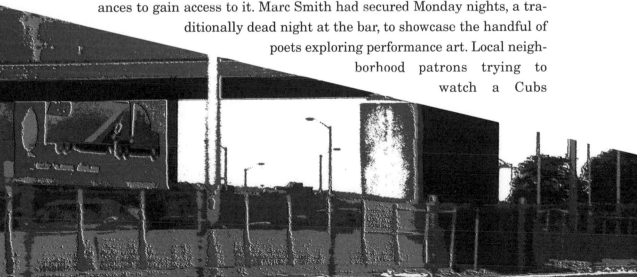

game and down a beer would find themselves being assaulted by poets utilizing wild gestures, musical instruments, boom boxes, costuming, and theatrical makeup. Some of the most memorable performances pieces there included Tim Anderson's performance piece about "butt-fucking in the cornfields" delivered with midwestern innocence and charm, ending in dropped-drawer-exposure, and David Cooper's "anyone call a cab?" with Cooper storming onto the stage as a perceived cab driver growing more impatient and violent by the minute.

My first performance of "Dollmaker" took place there, a performance piece delving into child abuse and addiction. These were simpler, shorter works. But as venues continued to open and offer space for alternative work, performance art, performance poetry, and experimental theater often merged and blossomed.

Of course, the performance poets that would become the Chicago Poetry Ensemble and start the slam at the Green Mill really had their first encounter together at David Jemilo's bar, the Déjà Vu. Again, Marc Smith arranged for a group of invited poets to perform there. This time, they created a collaborative performance piece based on a single concept: the voices of carnival and circus performers. The debut performance piece was called "Circus Chatter." The audience, to everyone's surprise, was totally engaged.

The success of "Circus Chatter" encouraged Jemilo to invite Smith to regularly feature performance poetry on Sunday nights at his new bar, the Green Mill, an historic speakeasy that showcased late-night jazz. This weekly opportunity created a great challenge since the Chicago Poetry Ensemble now had to develop a whole evening of performance poetry every week.

It was also an immense stimulus for greater development of work and artists. Inspired by the vital performance art activity in Chicago, and the con-

tinued opportunity to showcase work at the Green Mill, a more elaborate body of work began to appear: "Acts of Lunacy" and "Eating Meat" were my solo performance pieces with staging, projected images, and animal sound effects, the latter performed while sitting at a small table, dressed in white, lit only by candlelight, while eating a full, raw sirloin steak. Both poems alluded to imminent danger. Another work, "The Book Burning," which took place at the Guild Books space, ended with the audience participating in an actual book burning in the alley outside.

A more elaborate body of work, produced and directed by myself, incorporating dance (Pat Fischer Selby), performance poetry (Marc Smith, Dwight Okita, and myself), theater (Morgan McCabe) projection, lighting, body art, photography (Jeff Crissman), music, and sound, "Tattoo, Taboo" represented the historical, sexual, spiritual world of tattooing, and was received by sold-out audiences at the ARC Gallery. Marc Smith himself directed ensemble performance pieces for the Mill, such as "Dance" and "War." Many of these were more theatrical poetry productions with elements of performance art alive within them.

This early groundwork and, of course, the rising popularity of the slam, brought in a whole new school of performance poets, some such as Cin Salach, who collaborated with Mark Messing and others to create the performance art group, The Loofah Method, and Ten Tongues—successfully incorporated different media, including projection, music/sound creation, kinetics, and video.

The exploratory spirit of performance art and its sister, performance poetry, invites—actually it requires—constant innovation and change in order to reflect upon the audiences it hopes to engage.

worship
for emil kober

inhale when the glass invites me in, singing
swim through fire to save me, exhale
and hold perdition between my lips,
kiss god in the face of god and picture
old nick plump with pleasure, look up
profane, circle pew pulpit preacher penance,
believe all I need to turn temple into pagoda
is desire, repeat until the pope pops
in to see if I'm up for a little communion
but confess that I just ate the body of god
an hour ago so I'm really not hungry yet.

•

*people who pray in glass churches shouldn't
    worship stones.*
I've wanted to live in a glass house as long as I
    can remember. the idea of it thrilled me.
I had a million questions for my mom but got it
    down to three: would the bathroom be glass

too? could people see everything always or
would there be *one* place in the house that
wasn't glass? and what about when you
sleep—would people watch you dream?

•

the ocean in my body moves and the world rocks
    itself awake—rested, smooth, sleep shakes
    its hair loose falling open around my mouth
    making me an easy entrance for all visitors.
    it's a free day. the moon is handing out
    afternoon passes and this is not a fantasy
    but I dreamed it once while I was swimming
    through the lake pretending ocean and
    imagining water's entrance a billion airless
    doorways swinging wide from chicago to
    laguna the breathless caribbean the busy
    gulf and I was balancing my body on lake
    currents surfing right below the surface of

* You can hear Cin Salach performing Anne Sexton's "Music Swims Back to Me" on the audio CD (track 14).

me my line of flesh blood bone thinking fish
be fish slip through when the glass entered
my mind the crucible of sand 2000 degrees of
ambition and accidents and all my air floated
to the surface.

•

after gathering and marvering and blowing, after
reheating and blocking and necking, after filing
and tapping and transferring, after jaxing and
flashing and breaking this

•

stand back.
kneel.
enter yourself
like a house.

*

Evolution

It's Thursday and someone's testing the new
church bells
so every few minutes it's Sunday. God's in the air
and
out of the blue, I'm moved to begin tracking my
religion
in feathers   watch them float randomly down,
land randomly
here. Looking up to witness their journey, I'm
surprised how
far they've traveled in seven days. God's breath
sending them
down, establishing faith and gravity. A noticeable
pile has
collected at my feet. Proof we didn't crawl out of
the ocean
in the beginning. In the beginning we just fell out
of the sky,
squawking, flopping, wondering about the
architecture of
nests, looking for the right building materials and
something
to hold us all together. Something like skin. Or skin.

*

todd alcott

hear...

track 16

Television

Look at me. Look at me. Look at me, look at me, look at me. Look at me. No no no, don't look over there, there's nothing to look at over there, look at me, look at me, look at me.

Are you looking at me? Is everybody looking at me? Do I have your attention? Good.

Don't get the wrong idea. I'm not trying to take over your life. You need, what? What do you need? You need to, what? Go to the bathroom? Fine. Get up, go to the bathroom, come back, look at me. You need, what? You need to get something to eat? Fine. Get up, go to the kitchen, get something to eat, come back, look at me. You need to, what, sleep? Fine, get up, go to bed, go to sleep, get up, come back, look at me.

Okay. So we have an agreement. You will do what you *absolutely need to do,* and when you're done, you will come back and look at me.

Don't worry about your schedule. I am here for you. I am here for you. Twenty-four hours a day, seven days a week, I am here for you.

I am here for you. You need me, I'm here. Fair
and foul, thick and thin, I am here for you. I
am here for you. People try to tell you I'm
bad? You tell them that I am here for you.
Twenty-four hours a day, fair and foul, thick
and thin, I am here for you. I am here for you.
People try to tell you I'm bad, know what it
sounds like to me? Sour grapes.

You see what I—hey, hey, hey, hey, hey, no, don't
look over there, there's nothing going on over
there, look at me, look at me, look at me.

I've got stuff you wouldn't believe. Danger? Sex?
Action? Death? Thrills? Comedy? All here, all
in the next eight minutes.

Can you believe it? You can't. It's unbelievable.
You can't believe it <u>because it's unbelievable</u>!
It's a miracle.

Just keep looking at me. Just keep looking at me.
Just keep looking at me. Look at me, look at
me, look at me, look at me, look at me.

*

jean howard

Dancing in Your Mother's Skin
—For Ed Gein

Ed, you've been a naughty boy.
But who can tell what
darkness swims between
a young boy
and his mother?
Your little hands snug
as a cockle
around her fingers
now are claws
that dip right in.
An oceaned viscera
glistens in the wind
of the backyard shed.

Poor little Ed.
The hulk of your mother
on your back,
I, too, am ashamed to let
her near,
but crawl into her skin
at my every fear.

A gutless course we've taken here.
Moonlight trailing on the backporch screen.
Don't let me into
the heart that starts up after
midnight.
Don't let me sing
a vacant lullaby
with the buzz saw.

The line is thin
between a boy and all
the close-calls
that make him real.
Washing off the night's ink,
the bed is only a half-room
away.
But let it reel in its
pallid valor

for the moon is just right,
and you're dancing in your
mother's skin.

*

Dollmaker

I am involved
in the make-shift of dolls.
I can make heads
ugly as cauliflower.
Their arms grow from
needles,
those fucking, fucking forms
of cloth.

Their braids hang, yarn
gongs, as freaky
      as twins.
I am the maker
         of dolls.
Attentive and fluffy,
They love me. I am their mother.
Their parts are scattered
               everywhere.

*

Hemingway Afternoon

Wesleptwewokeweatewefuckedwesleptwewoke
    weatewefucked...
DarlingIloveyoudoyoulovemedarlingIloveyoudo
    youloveme...
IamamanlamamanlymanthemostmanlymanIam...
Closethomosexualclosethomosexualcloset
    homosexual...
Bullfightingbullfightingbullfightingbullfighting...
It was good.

*

Sirens at the Mill

The drone of online dulled a metal-sweet sleep
that made it painless to mop up melted time
and ring it into dumpster number one.

For me, the machine was easy.
It asked for nothing but reaction
and acquiescence to rhythm.
Sky-high wages for steel-toed idle?
No problem. So I worked with it.

And after a while
it was breath, it was beat,
brand new involuntary.
And as I locked on into patterns,
all I could do was listen:
to blue-blade harmonies, steel-braced downbeat,
repetita, repetita, repetita, repetita
in knife time.
It was nice.

I numbed and understood
how anyone could wear the grind,
lifer with a shard smile,
because the whole thing was habit and ritual.
And there's no place safer.

And then right in the middle of constant,
right next to rely, on top of depend,
there's this catch
on a ring that I wasn't supposed to be wearing.

There was time, I thought, for a laugh or two.
There was room I thought for a healthy
"Well fool, look what you did now,"
I mean there's always slack in my schedule.

Until I felt it:
The rip of penitence, pinch of metal press, crush
    of forward,
and old clichés stepped lively,
cold as a machine, thorough as a machine.
And I thought of my brother down at the Popsicle
    factory,
put his hand on a guardrail as a two-ton punch
    press
whistled millimeters from his fingers.

And I thought of my grandfather down at the
    Coca-Cola bottler,
he lost half of both his thumbs.
And you wonder where these scars come from,
from here, from now
here and now,
here and now
because it's not stopping, it won't stop.
And I can feel it pull absence of ice and itch of
    flame
and the smooth dry cross-grain of a man's back
and I know,
I know,
I know,
I know,
I know...
Until some slo-mo supervisor swam through
    nappy-time
and pushed a button;
gave me back a sense of gift,
tangible grace now,
one under which we flourish,
and one that I will not now
do without.

*

Performance art

blood, ice skates, and coyotes in the 20th century (by Gregory Harms)

"Where do we go from here?
Towards theater."
—John Cage

Over the course of the preceding century, the visual and fine arts underwent a transformation of such magnitude and severity as to surpass all preceding centuries. As the twentieth century saw not only the advent of new technologies—still and motion cameras, computers, et al.—it also witnessed a list of atrocities and international upheavals also great enough in magnitude to surpass preceding eras and epochs. This fast and bewildering emergence of modern life inspired artists to reconsider art's role in all forms and media. The same way the dawn of photographic technology caused artists to reconsider the role of painting in art—resulting in a redefinition that would eventually include the paint itself as the subject matter—so, too, did the exigencies, confusion, and novelty of the modern era cause artists to radically reconsider what the purpose of art was and, for the first time, *where* it should occur.

Performance art as an established idea, as something that we refer to as "performance art," had its genesis in the 1960s and 1970s. However, the art form has its underpinnings in the early twentieth century—from the mid-teens to the 1920s—when Dadaism was born in Europe. Serving as a reaction to the senseless and collective violence of World War I, Dadaism became a movement that encouraged the use of childlike spontaneity coupled with intellectual nihilism. Some renowned Dadaists included Tristen Tzara, Marcel Duchamp, Jean Arp, and Man Ray. Among other art forms, the Dadaists made films and engaged in performances, thus transmigrating art out of the gallery and museum to wherever seemed necessary. At mid-century, artists began to incorporate different—and oftentimes disparate—elements, creating an art form that, even today, has yet to be exhausted.

Lights, music, monologue, poetry, singing, screaming, televisions, fire, animals, dancing, film, blood: these are all a part of an extremely abridged list of elements that one might witness, or utilize, in a performance art piece. Some pieces last for zero minutes, zero seconds (John Cage's *0'00"*) while many have gone on for days and sometimes weeks. By the 1960s, performance art was completely underway and the *tabula rasa* created by the Dadaists' dismantling of art was fully being exploited.

Happenings and the Fluxus (Greek for "flowing") movement, both of which predominantly developed in America, were performance art movements that were inspired by the revolutionary experimentations of Jackson Pollock (painter) and John Cage (musician)—somewhat respectively, though Allan Kaprow was inspired by both artists when he began to create the concept of happenings in the late 1950s. Though Fluxus was somewhat of a minimalist reaction to happenings, they both pursued and realized the avant-garde endeavor to close the gap between art and lived life. Incorporating a wide variety of materials and media, happenings and Fluxus "concerts" attempted to re-engineer art into a mode of immediate communication through the deconstruction, manipulation, and reassembly of all art forms and their previously extant boundaries. During this period, one of the more noteworthy artists was Joseph Beuys (1921–1986), a German conceptualist, perhaps most famous for his *Coyote* performance. Beuys, who was loosely associated with Fluxus, removed himself from the movement, feeling that they "held a mirror up to people without indicating how to change anything." Others worth noting are Robert Rauschenberg, Claes Oldenburg, Nam June Paik, and Yoko Ono. Also during this period were a number of artists using themselves as their subject matter. Hermann Nitsch, of the Viennese actionists, used animal blood and the element of ritual to investigate catharsis and the psychological. Chris Burden, an American, used

self-mutilation as his subject and was perhaps most famous for having himself non-fatally shot in an art gallery.

Existing hitherto as a somewhat underground art form, performance art was elevated in production, appeal, and success by the Chicago-born Laurie Anderson. Born in 1947, Anderson started on the streets of New York performing simple pieces, most famously playing a violin and wearing ice skates encased in blocks of ice (*Duets on Ice*). By the late 1970s, Anderson was experimenting with sound, lighting, and narrative, culminating in her full-scale 1983 production, *United States* (a song from which, "O Superman," made its presence at the top of the British pop music charts). Most recently, she is known for her performance, *The Nerve Bible*, and her interpretive production of *Moby Dick*.

Another artist who emerged at the same time is the French performance artist, Orlan. Addressing issues of identity and beauty, Orlan (also born in 1947) has, since the 1970s, used plastic surgery and her own body as a medium through which to challenge beauty standards and conventions. Transforming her studio— the operating room—into theater, Orlan's performance-operations are filmed and photographed. Under local anesthetic, she reads from texts on psychoanalysis while her doctors, dressed in avant-garde fashions, transform her face and body, working from Renaissance iconography and, most recently, pre-Columbian Mesoamerican beauty conventions.

Throughout the late twentieth century, performance art has since moved in many directions and continues to metamorphose and manifest itself in different art forms. In pop and rock music, some early pioneers of incorporating performance art into their concerts include Syd Barrett (founding leader of Pink Floyd), David Bowie, and Alice Cooper. In the world of dance, the conceptualist, Bill T. Jones, throughout the '80s and '90s made innovative contributions to dance and choreography utilizing elements of costume, text, narrative, and video. Another experiment in performance was to remove altogether the human element, substituting it with mechanizations. Survival Research Laboratories, exploring—among other themes—sociopolitical satire, creates circus-styled arena events where large machines and robots tear one another apart in a spectacle of pyrotechnics and cacophony.

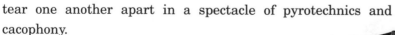

competitive poetry/taos

* part 4

(tracks 17–19)

introduction

By the late '70s and early '80s, poetry had become stale, the scene dried up. Performance art giving birth to performance poetry was one answer. Poetic boxing matches, another. And perhaps here again we find a seedling for the origins of today's poetic movement. While the idea of entertainment and "show" was the right format for poetry (a format that, in fact, resuscitated poetry), after the first couple of matches in Chicago, the scene relocated to Taos, New Mexico. Because of the beauty and rich poetic literary tradition, Taos developed into a hybrid of poetry "scenes." Leftover from the Beatnik era, high-ranking academic poets and slam poet crossovers were more the norm than the exception. Poet Daniel S. Solis is one such example. Firmly grounded in the aesthetics of the slam poetry scene, he also participated and helped maintain the wildness of the Taos Poetry Circus.

poetic Pugilism (by Terry Jacobus)

I have always been convinced that the best historians are the ones who live and record their history while they are alive only to "well-wish" that it won't be altered by historians of the future. Such is the futile world of records. In the microscopic world of contemporary poetic history over the past half-century there is a little and a lot at stake. The little is its long-term effect on the modern world. The lot is its effect on the individual spirits who are drawn and participate in the amorphous power of poetry.

In poetry, the payoff is mostly spiritual, and in most cases poetry may be the only art form where you pay to showcase your art. Poetry gives what you allow it to give and has a strong-willed aura unto itself that can maneuver experience, pleasure, and pain through a healing workout in the spoken air or on the page.

The stepladder into our new poetic millennium was preceded by a decade-dance that set the stage for an ancient/modern version of poetic presentation that would soon take hold.

The poetry world of the '50s was mostly dominated by the Beats, a breath of fresh air following prior years of rigid academic poetic rule. The gathering of this cluster of artists in New York headed by Jack Kerouac, Allen Ginsberg, William Burroughs, and Gregory Corso gripped their own iron fist over the poetry scene when their talents shook

Terry Jacobus
Al Simmons
7052 N. Damen
Chicago, Ill. 60645   May 18, 1982

Dear Terry Jacobus & Al Simmons,

I read a blurb about your poetry bouts in R

very interested. We're doing a poetry festival

Santa Fe the second & third weeks in August. Ma

"literal America" the way Elvis shook the bodies and minds of "young white America" with black blues and rock 'n' roll. The Beats' influence and national counterculture exposure still endure, but by the late '60s, especially in Chicago, things were slowly beginning to change.

In 1970, Northeastern Illinois University professor and playwright Alan Bates had the karmic insight to hire poet Ed Dorn as the university's next poet-in-residence. Ed was a brilliant instructor fresh from teaching at the University of Essex in Colchester, England. Ed was an aristocratic, active poet and a hands-on word sculptor, giving readings, having students over to his house, pushing the poetry envelope of their hearts and minds. Through Ed's connections, other poetry pros like Robert Creeley, Anne Waldman, Anselm Hollo, Philip Whalen, and Tom Raworth paraded through town with their talent, accessibility, and presence. After most of these readings at Northeastern's Creative Writing Center, we'd hang out at a bar or go back to Ed's house asking questions, interacting, learning, reaching new consciousness enhanced by chemistry and dialogue.

Thus sprouted an old idea in new minds, "Why don't we give poetry readings ourselves?" Set up a scene. There was certainly enough energy around with Ed's presence and inspiration setting tempo, purpose, and direction. So we formed a poetry gang called the "Stone Wind Poets" and ran a reading series out of the basement of a resale establishment called The Blue Store. The Blue Store was an un-Beat whiskey/coffeehouse hangout where you could vent passion and aggression. We had an open mic, featured readers and great basement debates. The Blue Store had a natural underground flavor and it survived for two years.

In the midst of all this poetry glee, wisdom, and energy, we occasionally observed and sensed—even in ourselves—an aura of unspoken competitiveness

Taos founder Peter Rabbit (Douthit) invites Jacobus to the Circus.

The tentative date for the Taos bout(we'll do two - one here, one in Santa Fe) is August 14. The prize money will be $500 to the Champion in each contest as well as a silver belt buckle. The audience will be the judge. The runner up will be compensated. All expenses (food & lodging) will be paid by the festival.

We're going ahead with this peculiar hype with you or without you so you might as well come. Have you got a satin robe?

Pinto beans & Spanish ricely yours,

Peter L. Douthit
Director
Taos Poetry Festival

between poets. With certain poetry pros, there was an invisible pretentious aura fogging the air—possibly freezing or stunning a student or poetry fan in his or her tracks. We figured it was just the yin and yang of the learning Earth curve, but at times, we were surprised by its avid intensity. So the seeds of Chicago poetry competitions were being sown in the reading scenes, party dialogues, and pretentious hubris that some "made" and "unmade" poets carried with them.

When Ed Dorn's residency ended, he suggested the hiring of poetry's Socrates, Ted Berrigan. A noted New York poet, a great ad-libber, boyishly tough with a creative competitive mind, Ted once said, "When I read with somebody I want to kick their ass!" With Ted's out-front competitiveness showing, he hit the sonnet on the head. It made tangible sense and left a mark. Let me be clear that a lot of the readings given during these years were amazing soul-sharing experiences, but there were just as many that were boring, self-indulgent, non-informative, dull presentations. Why couldn't poetry entertain as well as enlighten? Why couldn't poetry be accessible as well as intelligent? Of course, in my opinion, great work performs itself on or off the page. Great work on the page can produce a miraculous intimacy with the reader. A neurological one-on-one without the poet's oral voice. However, great work read or performed to its potential can transform a collective audience and take them to another level.

In the mid '70s, the University of Illinois at Chicago Circle campus and the Yellow Press (a small publishing company run by professor poets at UIC, such as Michael Anania and Bill Knott) picked up the poetic slack by beginning a reading series of their own. They too brought many poets into the Chi-Town city scene with the backing of Paul Carroll (of "Big Table" fame).

Their reading scene wasn't as wild as ours, but it did continue the parade of writers coming through. Although, I must mention that at one of their readings Robert Bly got hit in the face with a pie by a group of so called "surrealists" who said "there will be no reading tonight!" Then they began to dance around oddly, throwing multicolored confetti into the audience. They said they were protesting a translation Bly did of some of Neruda's poems.

Terry Jacobus

We thought it was a gag, but when Circle poet Richard Friedman tried to take the mic and restore order, he was choked off the stage. So some of the Stone Wind poets attending (Al Simmons, Henry Kanabus, and myself) went to work. A huge fight ensued and spilled out onto Lincoln Avenue. We did some pretty good pounding before Chicago's finest showed up, and my friends and I almost got arrested for poetry. Arrested for poetry? Pretty cool. So as the "surrealists" fled, the Bly reading finally proceeded.

By the late '70s, the Circle scene ended and there was a poetic dead energy filling the Disco air. The hip poets in residence moved on and the young poets and writers grew up into teachers, bus drivers, editors, ad agents, tenured academicians, salesmen, or clerks. The magic energy dissolved, and the sphere broke apart.

But the world of poetry has it own resolve, to paraphrase poet Anselm Hollo: we poets are an invisible legion, charging into the valley of death like the six hundred, shouting "dig it!"

In 1980, Stone Wind poet Al Simmons was tending bar in a club in the Lincoln Park/DePaul University area. At the time, two artists were having a heated disagreement about their work. Apparently, Jim Desmond and Jerome Sala didn't like each other or each other's work, or both. It was the poets' art war rearing its literal, physical head.

Al Simmons, with the experience of his poetic past, picked up on the confrontation and said to me, "I should do 'poetry bouts.' Let 'em put up or shut up. We'll have judges, a boxing ring, ring girls, etc. We'll give the aggression a format to work its way out and possibly make some money."

"That's goofy," I initially replied. "An insult to the art." But then I thought about the active metaphor and the seditious competitiveness of the past, and agreed it was a brilliant idea. A poetic manifestation of Ted Berrigan's "kick their ass" comment.

o II

erry
pe told me
ou hello.
lians wept to
r great I was
and Yeytushenko
I me and said
lations, Ted!"
gave me some
Bogary Crso
ordan, beats)

LOZZI - ROMA
SH OF OTTAWA
m my own cake, love, Ted

Terry Jaco
7057 N. Dar
Chi. Illino
U.S.A.

I volunteered to do color commentary for the first bout with Chicago poet Gerry Czerwien, and helped commissioner Simmons line up some hot female personnel as ring girls.

Through consultation with friends, the World Poetry Association (WPA) was formed with Simmons as commissioner, and with that, the Zoom was on.

In the spring of 1981, Simmons ran his first "Poetry Bout." It was a three-fight card which featured punk poet Jerome Sala vs. blues man Jim Desmond—the bar fighting boys—to determine who would be the first Heavyweight Poetry Champion. It was a ten-round fight, poem vs. poem, song vs. verse, scored on the WPA's ten-point must system: ten points to the winner of a round, nine or less to the loser. It took place at a Hubbard Street loft and was billed as the WPA's "Main Event" Poetry Fights.

The overall ambience of this activity was like a cockfight north of the border. The poetry scene was oozing with a new raw nervous energy that buzzed the room. Sala emerged the victor in a close intense battle, although as color man, I don't recall any "intellectual knockdowns." The overall event was a success.

At the time of the first bout and all through the '80s, I was the Chicago correspondent for *Rolling Stock* magazine, a literary periodical started by Ed and Jennifer Dunbar Dorn and backed by the University of Colorado.

I reported on this first bout and it made *Rolling Stock's* front page. Peter Rabbit, a veteran influential poet, entrepreneur, and ex-commune headmaster, read the article and sent me a letter asking whether Al Simmons would like to take his bout show to New Mexico and make it national by including it as part of a "poetry circus" in Taos.

Before a final decision was made, Al ran two more bouts in 1981: one at the No Exit bar near Chicago's Old Town, and the other at Tuts, a club not too far from Wrigley Field. Sala remained champion as the crowds and intense craziness grew. When Al asked Sala if he wanted to take his championship to New Mexico, Sala refused because he was ready to get married and move to New York, taking on a real-world advertising job. Al then asked me if I wanted to do it, and after some deliberation, I agreed.

THE MAIN EVENT
World Championship Poetry Bout
Terry Jacobus vs. Gregory Corso

produced by Al Simmons
in conjunction with SOMOS

Max Finstein Memorial Trophy

Peter Rabbit and his wife, Anne MacNaughton, made their National Champion Gregory Corso, of beatnik fame. Gregory called himself "Captain Poetry," and with his buddies Allen Ginsberg and Peter Orlovsky, they could possibly draw a decent crowd. So they had a National Champ of reputation and I became the challenger to take him on. I was actually looking forward to it because I was tired of the Beats' poetic domination and getting most of the coast-to-coast recognition, plus being a local Chicago kid myself, nothing would give me more pleasure than taking on a New York beatnik and possibly winning a National Title for the Second City....but I knew it wasn't going to be easy.

Here is an excerpt from a pre-fight hype interview I did for *Rolling Stock* with Commissioner Simmons just before the first national bout:

Terry Jacobus: What's the World Poetry Association? (WPA)

Al Simmons: It's nothing.

TJ: What do you mean, it's nothing?

AS: Just that, it's nothing.

TJ: Then what purpose does it serve?

AS: It's a means unto itself.

TJ: That sounds metaphysical.

AS: Maybe it is.

TJ: I need a definition.

AS: Okay, the WPA is an organization developed for the sole purpose of supplying itself with a legitimacy of form in order to establish a criteria of standards, regulations, and rules to govern a literary sporting event.

TJ: Do you think the "poetry world" is competitive?

AS: I think poets are competitive. When you're reading with someone you'd like to think you stole the show. My fights are based on this basest form.

TJ: Oh.

So in August 1982, the WPA and I headed for Taos, New Mexico, to take part in the first Poetry Circus and Taos's first heavyweight poetry bout.

Taos is a place full of God and shrouded in a multicultural population full of deep history, religion, magic, rituals, and spells. It paints a backdrop of earth poetry itself, a tan meditation close to the earth. It was and is the perfect setting for literary action. The World Heavyweight Poetry Championship was to be held on Saturday, August 14, 1982, as the climax event after a week of readings and poetry activities that preceded it.

With an introductory presentation that evening that included Allen Ginsberg and Peter Orlovsky, Gregory Corso and I prepared to do battle. And what a battle it was! Corso and I barbed it out in a packed auditorium as PBS cameras rolled. Gregory, with classic prima donna whining, kept interrupting me as I tried to read my work, pleading with Ginsberg in the audience that he wasn't doing anything wrong. "Who put me with this fuckah? That isn't poetry, you're just saying something," Corso interjected as I read. Pretty good line, I thought, and tried to continue. I began the poem again. Yet again, Gregory interrupted me, yelling to Allen Ginsberg, "Allen, am I being a jerk?" Ginsberg's response from the audience: "Gregory, do whatever you want." Finally I responded, "Hey, in Chicago at least we give people an even chance."

Corso's reply: "I'm the daddy of poetry, did you know I was in Lucky Luciano's cell in '47? Did you know that?"

I'd finally had it, and spontaneously responded by pointing a finger right at him, "Hey, in '47 I wasn't born, and I was a god!"

It turned the tide. The audience realized I wasn't afraid, and my aggressive spontaneity as well as my poems were hitting home.

In the tenth and final round, I read a poem focused right at Corso and the Beats. It was titled "I Hear There Are Poets Here" and was based on a scolding, sloshed reading Gregory gave at an audience in Chicago in the late '70s. My poem ended with the line, "poets that'll kill if they have to." Gregory's response, "That's a beauty."

It was the final straw that broke the Beat poet's back, and as much as they possibly wanted Gregory and his entourage to return the following year, the judges ruled in my favor.

Al Simmons

So in the Land of Enchantment, I became the First World Heavyweight Poetry Champion, taking home "The Max," a sculptured boxing glove trophy designed by Linda Fleming and named after poet Max Finstein. In the immortal words of Ralph Kramden as he was about to be named "Raccoon of the Year," I wondered, "Am I worthy of such an honor?" My good angel told me "yes," so I was satisfied.

I kept the title through the '82–'83 poetic season until in defense of my crown I was defeated by poet-journalist Lewis MacAdams. Even though two out of the three judges voted for me, for some reason they added the scores collectively. It was bout "weirdness" at its best, but I flew home confident the true title still rested safely on my mantlepiece.

Once the fights took off in Taos, Peter Rabbit and his wife Anne MacNaughton cut a deal with Commissioner Simmons to keep the WPA bout format in the Poetry Circus, which now celebrates its twentieth year. Past Champions include Andrei Codrescu; Victor Hernandez Cruz; Anne Waldman; Quincy Troupe, Jr.; Ntozake Shange; Jimmy "Santiago" Baca; Simon Ortiz; and four-time retired champ Sherman Alexie. When Sherman stepped down, there was a runoff bout between two top contenders, Saul Williams of *Slam* movie fame and Pat Payne, a protégé of former champ Quincy Troupe, Jr. Pat won the title, and was one of three women to capture the crown since its inception in 1982.

Through the efforts of Peter Rabbit, Anne MacNaughton, Amalio Madueno, and others, the Taos Poetry Circus has been a wonderment of poetry classes, readings, slams, open readings, and, of course, the World Heavyweight Poetry Championship. The heavyweight bout reading alone always draws at least one thousand people. A thousand people for poetry? Good gosh! But it was true. And still is.

In Chicago, in 1985, I saw a major article in the *Chicago Tribune* featuring Marc Smith, a poet, skilled performance artist, and gifted master of ceremonies who was putting on poetry competitions called "Slams" at the Green Mill Lounge, a landmark jazz bar in Chicago's Uptown area. These weekly Slams exploded on the national scene and spread like wildfire from state to state, with teams and individuals from all over the country competing and creating performance

poetry like never before. "Slam" even became a poetry cultural catchword that replaced "Beat" in the vernacular of the common poetic mindset. Both "bout" and "slam" gave inspiration and dedication to those who cared to compete, or those who just chose to listen and be entertained. Both gave major shots of excitement, seriousness, and folly to an art form that sometimes lacked an edge. Also, unlike some of the pomposity of the academy, it brought poetry back to the street in massive doses. Through bouts and slams, Chicago was at the root of a performance poetry revolution, giving a huge adrenaline shot in the arm to an art form that touches youth from a different angle, and gets poetry followers and activists involved in an engaging atmosphere.

As Peter Rabbit and Anne MacNaughton discovered in the chemistry of their Taos poetry nights, if you call a poetry reading a "reading," you never know how many will show. If you call a poetry gathering a "competition," they will come. And they still do.

As Marc Smith learned through his persistence and experience, if you add the word "Slam" to a poetry venue in any state, you will pack them in. In either case, poetry still breathes, and in either case, poetry wins.

terry jacobus

track 19

So Edgar Allan Poe Was in this Car

So Edgar Allan Poe was in this car goin' the wrong way on ol' 66 and it's snowin' hard and he's pissed off and worried about everything so he manages to pull over to the side and his woman gets outta the car to check out the situation but Edgar won't get out and his woman realizes that he isn't gettin' out so she goes to wunna them phone stands near a big pole by the Wrong Way sign and calls up his good friend Sam Coleridge and Sam says "Okay, hold on, I'll be right out there." Well Sam gets there in pretty good time and he sees Edgar just sittin' there locked in with his arms crossed and his face stern, hard glazed and sorta mean...So Sam starts bangin' on the window sayin,' "Com'on out man, get it together, you've got a lot to do yet and you've got a hot woman and a lot goin' for ya, plus I'm interested enough to come all the way down here to get ya cause you're my good friend and all." But Poe turned his head real slow and stiff-like and he glared right at Sam between the glass and his expression never changed when he says, "Look man I've got a fuckin' raven in the back seat of this car and he never leaves wherever I am and I'm sick of all this shit and havin' to write it down cause that's all I can do with it!"

So Sam pleads with him somemore givin' him comfort about his plight as well as platitudes about his work, an people are lookin' and passin' by in common cars and some of them got kids in the back seat and they're laughin' while Poe's woman is sitting near the side of the highway crying, hoping and concerned. Then after ten minutes or so of this goin' on

Coleridge gets tee'd off himself and starts
rantin' and ravin' and runnin' in circles around
Poe's car real fast then real slow then real
fast again and he's flappin' his arms and bitin'
his lips until he rips off his coat and his shirt
and all at the same time flings himself in front
of Edgar's windshield and says, "You Asshole!
You're so worried about that damn raven in
your car well take a look at this thing!" And
there about Sam's neck hung an eighty-
pound albatross like a huge noxious pendant.
And Poe looked at it close and saw it was
real. So he unhooked the button on his sedan
and got out of the car and Poe's woman got
up, straightened her dress and stopped
crying, cause she was glad
It was over for this time.

*

I Hear There Are Poets Here

I hear there are poets here!
Corso on the Tree of Woe
came out sneering in Chicago
as if Jack's prose hadn't
made them all
and what could you say
knowledge doesn't come easy
it's laced with snakeskin
and snarls at you
with its yellow teeth
and strangling eyes
tells you you'd better get
out of the way
unless you call it out
into the street
to take a shot
in the jungle cities
where the beatily bop
Beats did play
holding on to their time
like it would go away
and it will
and our time too will fade

Lost/Glorious/Abandoned/Hollow
Serene
the Human scream
changes with experience
and the stakes are high
and instinctually planted
cause there's a game out there
everyone's tellin' you about
the Inside Show/The Outside Play

everyone's tellin you about sitting
and self as if there aren't enough
dead American egos
floundering around our hemisphere
as if the East is gonna save us
when they can't even save themselves
as if we don't have enough myths
of our own to cling on to
like Space/Leisure/or the Film

Be careful, too much knowledge
makes the man mean
makes the woman spiteful
forces the world to predictably
expect its own doom

dancing under a mushroom of love
a poet now snarls
I hear there are Poets here!

Poets with the guts to pay the price
of the sound, the spear and the
endless competition

Poets that'll kill if they have to!

*

Terry Jacobus

door
lead me in a prayer
headed for the open heart
when you are ready
you will see us all
one spirit at a time
it may take an eternity
but I'll be patient
it's worth the wait

*

Patience

those who love for god
and those who kill for god
expect to land
on the same plane as god
dear god, even if you are
nothing
hold me tight tonight
breathe me in a womb
and hold me to the light
kiss me like the fool
kisses for love
take me the way a soul
slides through the peaceful

The Fight Game

I love that kinky shit
Can't get it offa my mind.
Mike Tyson fought Larry Holmes
For the Heavyweight Championship of the World.

Two men
Face to Face.
Alone.

Don King is my guru.
Mike Tyson is the greatest
Muhammed Ali was the greatest.
Have you seen him lately?
Poet and avatar.

I looked in the mirror
And saw the Manassa Mauler's swollen face.
The Brown Bomber.
Rocky Marciano.
Sugar Ray and Sugar Ray.
Marvelous Marvin and the Hit Man.
Hands of Stone, Manos de Piedra.

Stand up there and take your beating.
Another comeback
Till the brain is soft and amorphous,
Lips battered out of control.
"Float like a butterfly,
Sting like a bee."
A pit bull in the closet.

Where are the Russians?
Can one of them take Iron Mike?
Can anybody quit while they're still quick?
The Shadows accumulate.
We are each in our turn knocked out.

Sports Teams

That gets us to sports teams & their names.
Ain't no redskins playing pro ball,
ain't no Vikings or Celtics.

Reflecting players the Browns are
the only team with an honest name.
Reflecting demographics
it's gotta be the Washington Jigaboos,
San Francisco Cocksuckers,
Seattle Slopes, San Antonio Spics,
New York Yids, Atlanta Yard Apes.

This is a left handed prayer
ladies and gentleman, boys and girls,
that we may finally learn
to see beyond the surface,
beyond appearance,
a brother or sister
reflected in every eye.
We gotta love everybody.

*

Peter Rabbit

Welcome to the Revolution

I was,
walking the University of New Mexico
under the pines
cutting through the perfect mountain air
searching the shadows
for the bloodstains
from the riots.
Student led anti-war demonstrations
when "Mexican-American" Guardsman
bayonneted Chicano students
having traded obsidian blade
and Toledo steel
for
oiled and honed army issue
in fixed position
point and thrust
and the blood blossomed from earth brown skin.
And that was less than thirty years ago
and I was tracking down those puddles
so I could put my fingers into them
like some kind of
coagulated
Holy water

blood pudding.
And maybe I could put in my thumb
and pull out a heart
Cem-Anahuac-City of the Aztecs
heart of the one world
beating
like a gory jewel
in the undulating copper sun of my dreams
and I lost focus
closed my eyes
vertigo unfolding
when a hand gripped my shoulder
hard.
I opened my eyes and there he was,
in the dream flesh,
Cesar Chavez,
el mero-mero de el Movimiento Chicano.
"Pos, que diablos tienes, bato?" he asks
and I think,
my dance card of demons is way too long to list
but before I can answer
he punches me in the gut
a beautiful right that knocks me on my ass

he stands over me radiating
that terrible sweet saint's intensity
eyes pools of onyx fire,
glittering love,
and destruction.
"I thought you were non-violent!" I gasp.
"You call that violence?" he asks, sincerely
    amused and appalled.
"The only violence here is your immense
    ignorance pendejo!
Dip your fingers into the dried up blood of
    students? What crap!
Why not go for fresh blood?
Dip your fingers into the blood of Zapatistas
    dying in the Jungles of Chiapas.
Dip your fingers, hands, into the shattered
    dreams of immigrants being hounded
by the border patrol, coyotes and la Migra.
Dip your fingers, hands arms into all of the
    sangre Chicano being spilled by gangs
the cops and clicas in the streets and callejones
    of Dallas, Chicago, L.A. and Albuquerque...
you think it stopped flowing
just because the P.B.S. special ended?
just because you quit thinking about it?
just because there was no one around to yell
    'VIVA LA RAZA!'
and wake your big ass up?"
He grabbed my face and shoved it into a mirror
    and said
"That's violence! Everyday you don't speak the
    language of your Grandmothers
and your Grandmothers' Grandmothers, that's
    violence!"

and I knew
he was right
and I turned to him,
but he was gone.
And in his place
was Santos Rodriguez,
a wavering twelve year old angel
with half his head blown away by the Dallas
    police
and I trembled—
as he took my hand
and we took flight,
rose into the air,
and we flew backwards,
past the L.A. riots
smoke and fire licked at us
and we rose higher,
screams from furnace heat napalms victims Viet
    Nam
and we rose higher
Mexico City 1968, students machine gunned in
    the bloody streets
and we rose higher....
All the way to a valley in northern Mexico

Daniel S. Solis

at the beginning of the last century
where the La Cucaracha,
the troops of Pancho Villa were encamped.
Where,
Adelitas,
Amazonian Mestizas
of legendary courage and ferocity sat,
oiling rifles, honing machetes.
While the men,
prepared atole tortillas and tamales.

Unself-concious role reversal
because revolution is more important than
    machismo.
And Santos sets me down face to face
with el General, Francisco Villa
and he is grinning with a humor full of danger
and in the silence I realize
that everyone is staring at me,
waiting...
and Villa's face
changes
to the face of a child
waiting,
to be taught
to read
in English
and Spanish.
and a voice in my head says,
"Welcome to the revolution, cabroooon!"

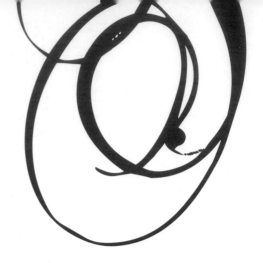

Elephant Song

"KILLER ELEPHANT RAMPAGES HONOLULU !"
the headline said.

At first I thought it was a joke,
the elephant caught in front page ink,
gaudy circus head gear still in place,
Then,
I saw the streaks of blood,
death's red fingers
wrapped
around another fleshy frame.

The next morning my friend Ethan
tells me of his landlady
5:30 a.m. ancient with tubes sticking out of her
    nose,
"HEY SONNY! look down the road there and see
if you don't see a cow!"
He looks.
No cow.
He thinks, she's losing it!

Cruising searchlight cops question,
"Hey buddy, you haven't seen a a cow pass by
    here have ya?"
Ethan shakes his head.
"Well a cow just came off the highway, and we
    think he's
around here somewhere."
Ethan reasons, a cow, fresh off the highway,
would go to a cow rest stop.
He flicks on his headlights into what used to be
    Thomas Wolfe's back yard
to be met by a bovine glare,
defiant of ropes
and slaughter houses.
Skittish brown outlaw cow skeedaddles!
Into the 6 a.m. dark...

and somewhere,
elephants in cages
dream of the veldt.
and wake
to forgetting
and forced drudgery.
But,
one elephant,
remembered
the vivid dream,
not gray but green
unencumbered foraging green
cool water, antelopes dart away green
ears flapping, take a long drink,
eyes closed cause not even lions will fuck with
    me green
the dream,
huge and wrinkled...

Awake now,
awake.
Wanting,
luaus and orchids for dessert,
wanting,
waterfalls,
wanting,
naps in the afternoon sun.
Eyes alight with the thought of wading into the
    ocean,

the ocean...

But, the trainer could not understand
could not grasp this
little kid amusement park excitement.
He responded with iron bar
with hook and tugs
and clipped commands
and finally panic —
as pachydermic efforts
to shake him awake into the dream,
broke his,
fragile
frightened
grip on life.

Then down the street
into the morning,
a few injured accidentally
it would have been so easy to kill,
you know
strong as an elephant and all.

And as elephantine joy
turned to cacaphonous sorrow and confusion
    jumbled rage,
no one
nothing
understood.
the sunlight
standing mute and stupid.
the people
running
screaming
falling.
the uncomprehending concrete
constant redundant
then—
eleven bullets.
eleven holes punched by police rifles.
pack dogs reliable and rote
in their capacity to destroy.
Eleven holes,
punched into the dreaming gray canvas.
Like the eleven stars Vincent used
to puncture the blue night-time sky.

the moon groaning orange in its cracked cage
and the dream
runs red
in the gutter
again.

But,
I will slip away,
and dive into that water green evening.
I will remember
the blue morning of a dangerous cow on the
    loose
in downtown Asheville
dodging stolid cops and nosy old ladies.
I will remember,
the graceful lumbering dream
galloping bright eyed
across the veldt
forever...

*

The taos Poetry circus

(by Anne MacNaughton)

The handful of poets who began the Taos Poetry Circus twenty years ago founded a three-ring festival dedicated to widening the experience of the spoken word. In the space of a week, it celebrates all that poetry is and more, for it focuses on the oral presentation, and this makes it unique.

To experience a poem "spoken" by the poet is to be present at the moment of creation, for once a poem has been composed, "written," the energy of its creation is accessible anew each time it's spoken aloud. For the audience, this shared experience is also an intimate connection with the poet (a word whose etymological root is "maker") as the poem is created in the listener's mind in the moment of its pronouncement. As former World Heavyweight Champion Poet Anne Waldman declares, "Something always occurs." The power of the performance of poetry occurs when one beholds a work of language art just as it's breathed out into the air.

When asked why Taos, a tiny and remote village in the northern mountainous regions of the desert Southwest, is a site for the burgeoning event, I respond by referring to the roots of the oral literary tradition in this area. It is in part because of this remoteness that the rural folk have retained some of the ancient oral traditions, not the least of which can be experienced every winter in most New Mexico villages.

This is the season when folk poetry flourishes, from prehistoric Zuñi where priests' ancient chants recreate the world in houses of the night-long Shalako ceremony, to northern Hispanic villages where men on horseback shout rhymed lines of archaic Spanish in the caballo-drama, the historic epic, *Los Comanches*. Where

dances from the days of mountain *genizaro* and Plains traders are presented in the snow each January first, processing 'round the village by pickup truck. Where Spanish songs are sung in praise before doorways, verses improvised in the space of a guitar stanza, to honor the resident. Or where Spanish descendants and indigenous villagers alike keep alive *Los Matachines*, a medieval dance-drama, layered with myth, legend, numerology, several world religions, music, and poetic metaphor.

As Peter Rabbit has stated about first coming to Taos: "When I got here in the middle 1950s Mabel Dodge and company featuring D.H. Lawrence had already put Taos on the literary map. Ed Dorn did a residency up at the Lobo [D.H. Lawrence] Ranch. Robert Creeley was around. We were young and vigorous. It was good to be a poet in Taos." After the 1960s counterculture types and community dwindled into the late 1970s, "the literary scene was low energy. We staged readings and nobody came. Phil Whalen draws ten people. Jimmy Santiago Baca, Miguel Piñero, Miguel Algarín, and Lucky Cienfuegos…incredible art, but with no audience, it's wasted, gone on the wind. We read in the Dorns' *Rolling Stock* of poetry fights that were happening in Chicago. So, in 1982 we created the Taos Poetry Circus, invited Allen Ginsberg, Gregory Corso, and Peter Orlovsky to come perform. The 'Main Event' was between Gregory Corso and Terry Jacobus, a young veteran of the Chicago poetry wars. Jacobus won the title by TKO when Corso was overwhelmed by the extreme lunacy of the event and Jacobus's aggressive tactics. The transcendental readings, outdoors with music on Sunday at the San Geronimo Lodge to a sizable audience, convinced us we should do it again. We attracted modest crowds. We were in the poetry business."

Poetic orality is not a novelty here. It exists in the soul of rural New Mexico, an organic connection to its long past. And the beauty of the shared experience of listening transforms those who attend events at the Poetry Circus, not unlike the shared effect of a spiritual experience.

We set out to offer the center stage to more voices of the misnamed "minorities" in this country, as well as to acknowledge that the heart of modern American poetry lies not in academic connection to the Old World as much as in the bubbling cauldron of the New. Our roots are native, in the Beat world, in the urban school, in the particular voice of America that uses numerous tongues. And now we influence the Old Worlds with our words, our poetic culture rises to the standards of those of the older civilizations. Oh Walt Whitman, we say to the originator of the American idiom, now we are heard in the world!

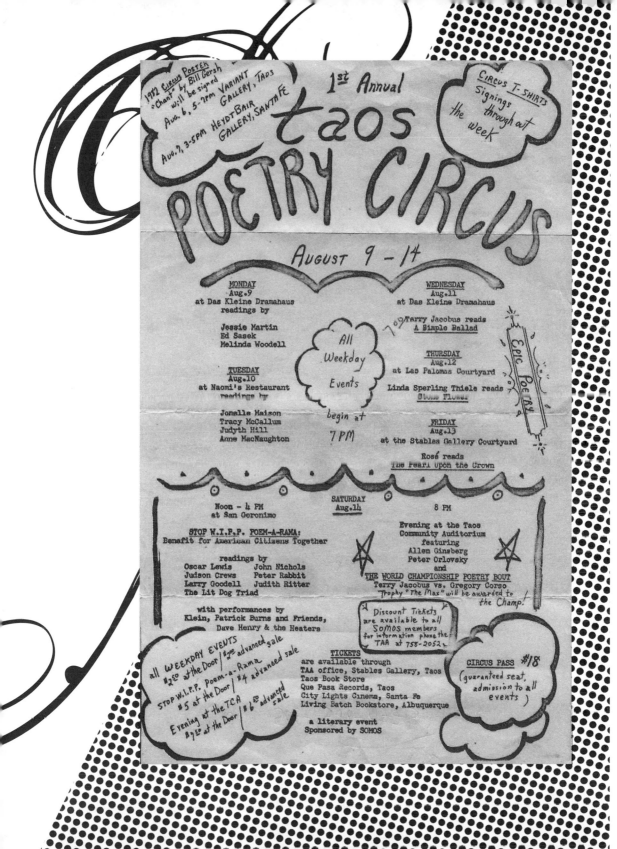

sherman alexie

Defending Walt Whitman

Basketball is like this for young Indian boys, all
    arms and legs
and serious stomach muscles. Every body is
    brown!
These are the twentieth-century warriors who will
    never kill,
although a few sat quietly in the deserts of
    Kuwait,
waiting for orders to do something, do
    something.

God, there is nothing as beautiful as a jump shot
on a reservation summer basketball court
where the ball is moist with sweat
and makes a sound when it swishes through the
    net
that causes Walt Whitman to weep because it is
    so perfect.

There are veterans of foreign wars here,
whose bodies are still dominated
by collarbones and knees, whose bodies still
    respond
in the ways that bodies are supposed to respond
    when we are young.

Every body is brown! Look there, that boy can run
up and down this court forever. He can leap for a
    rebound
with his back arched like a salmon, all meat and
    bone
synchronized, magnetic, as if the court were a
    river,
as if the rim were a dam, as if the air were a
    ladder
leading the Indian boy toward home.

Some of the Indian boys still wear their military
    haircuts
while a few have let their hair grow back.
It will never be the same as it was before!
One Indian boy has never cut his hair, not once,
    and he braids it
into wild patterns that do not measure anything.
He is just a boy with too much time on his hands.
Look at him. He wants to play this game in bare
    feet.

God, the sun is so bright! There is no place like
    this.
Walt Whitman stretches his calf muscles
on the sidelines. He has the next game.
His huge beard is ridiculous on the reservation.
Some body throws a crazy pass and Walt
    Whitman catches it with quick hands.
He brings the ball close to his nose
and breathes in all of its smells: leather, brown
    skin, sweat, black hair,
burning oil, twisted ankle, long drink of warm
    water,
gunpowder, pine tree. Walt Whitman squeezes
    the ball tightly.
He wants to run. He hardly has the patience to
    wait for his turn.
"What's the score?" he asks. He asks, "What's
    the score?"

Basketball is like this for Walt Whitman. He
    watches these Indian boys
as if they were the last bodies on earth. Every
    body is brown!
Walt Whitman shakes because he believes in
    God.
Walt Whitman dreams of the Indian boy who will
    defend him,
trapping him in the corner, all flailing arms and
    legs
and legendary stomach muscles. Walt Whitman
    shakes

because he believes in God. Walt Whitman
    dreams
of the first jumpshot he will take, the ball arcing
    clumsily
from his fingers, striking the rim so hard that it
    sparks.
Walt Whitman shakes because he believes in
    God.
Walt Whitman closes his eyes. He is a small man
    and his beard
is ludicrous on the reservation, absolutely
    insane.
His beard makes the Indian boys laugh
    righteously.
His beard frightens the smallest Indian boys.
    His beard tickles the skin
of the Indian boys who dribble past him. His
    beard, his beard!

God, there is beauty in every body. Walt Whitman
    stands
at center court while the Indian boys run from
    basket to basket.
Walt Whitman cannot tell the difference between
offense and defense. He does not care if he
    touches the ball.
Half of the Indian boys wear T-shirts damp with
    sweat
and the other half are bareback, skin slick and
    shiny.
There is no place like this. Walt Whitman smiles.
Walt Whitman shakes. This game belongs to him.

*

Song of Ourself

While Walt Whitman sang about his body, the still
     body
of one Indian grew into two, then ten, then
     multitudes.

*

Sherman Alexie

Totem Sonnets

1

Meryl Streep
Emily Dickinson
Dian Fossey
Flannery O'Connor
John Steinbeck
Helen Keller
Walt Whitman
Bruce Springsteen

Kareem Abdul-Jabbar
Zora Neale Hurston
Frida Kahlo
Pablo Neruda
Harriet Tubman
Muhammad Ali

2

Steamed Rice
Whole Wheat Bagel
Egg White
Baked Chicken

Tomato Soup
Broccoli
Cheddar Cheese
Garlic Clove

Grape Nuts and Non-Fat Milk
Almonds
Apple
Ice Water

Insulin
Hypodermic

3
Crazy Horse
Sitting Bull
Captain Jack
Black Kettle
Ishi
Joseph
Qualchan
Wovoka

Anna Mae Aquash
Wilma Mankiller
Tantoo Cardinal
Winona LaDuke
Buffy Sainte-Marie
Maria Tallchief

4
The Exorcist
Manhunter
Alien
Halloween

Star Wars
Escape from New York
Silent Running
Terminator

Little Big Man
Enter the Dragon
The Searchers
The Wild Bunch

Midnight Cowboy
The Graduate

5
Buddy Holly
Joni Mitchell
The Beatles
Janis Joplin
Hank Williams
Patsy Cline
The Ramones
Lou Reed

Robert Johnson
Sippie Wallace
Charley Paton
Memphis Minnie
Jaybird Coleman
Muddy Waters

6
Lenny
Edgar Bearchild
Holden Caulfield
Tess

The Misfit
Sula
Mazie
Tayo

Cacciato
Cecelia Capture
Hamlet
Jim Loney

Daredevil
The Incredible Hulk

7

Jesus Christ
Adam
Mary Magdalene
Eve

Jim Thorpe
Billy Mills
Billie Jean King
Ann Meyers

John Lennon
D.B. Cooper
Amelia Earhart
Martin Luther King, Jr.

Mother
Father

Marriage

What it comes to is this: bread.
Its creation the product of hunger and imagination.
We forget about it until we see it again on the table.
Tribes have gone to war because of wheat and
    corn.
When it is all you have to eat, there is never
    enough.
A sad day, when you realize the difference
    between good and bad bread.
Who first saw its possibilities?
If you feed enough to a bird, its stomach will
    explode. True or false?

Every culture is measured by its bread.
My mother makes her prodigal bread only when I
    visit.
It has always been meal for the poor and
    afterthought for the rich.
I walk by a bakery and realize why smell is the
    most important sense.
Sunday mornings we wash it down with coffee,
    then swallow it dry
as Eucharist that afternoon.
The sacred and utilitarian share an apartment
    overlooking the river.

*

Inside Dachau

1. big lies, small lies

Having lied to our German hosts about our plans
for the day, Diane and I visited Dachau
instead of searching for rare albums in Munich.
Only a dozen visitors walked through the camp
because we were months away from tourist
    season.
The camp was austere. The museum was simple.

Once there, I had expected to feel simple
emotions: hate, anger, sorrow. That was my plan.
I would write poetry about how the season
of winter found a perfect home in cold Dachau.
I would be a Jewish man who died in the camp.
I would be the ideal metaphor. Munich

would be a short train ride away from hell.
    Munich
would take the blame. I thought it would all be
    simple
but there were no easy answers inside the camp.
The poems still took their forms, but my earlier
    plans

seemed so selfish. What could I say about
      Dachau
when I had never suffered through any season

inside its walls? Could I imagine a season
of ash and snow, of flames and shallow graves?
      Munich
is only a short train ride away from Dachau.
If you can speak some German, it is a simple
journey which requires coins and no other plans
for the day. We lied about visiting the camp

to our German hosts, who always spoke of the
      camp
as truthfully as they spoke about the seasons.
Dachau is still Dachau. Our hosts have made no
      plans
to believe otherwise. As we drove through
      Munich
our hosts pointed out former Nazi homes, simply
and quickly. "We are truly ashamed of Dachau,"

Mikael said, "but what about all the Dachaus
in the United States? What about the death
      camps
in your country?" Yes, Mikael and Veronika, you
      ask simple
questions which are ignored, season after
      season.
Mikael and Veronika, I'm sorry we lied about
      Munich
and Dachau. I'm sorry we lied about our plans.

Inside Dachau, you might believe winter will
      never end. You might
lose faith in the change of seasons

because some of the men who built the camps
      still live in Argentina,
in Washington, in Munich.
They live simple lives. They share bread with
      sons and daughters
who have come to understand the master plan.

2. history as the home movie

it begins and ends with ash, though we insist
on ignoring the shared fires in our past.
We attempt to erase our names from the list
that begins and ends with ash.

We ignore the war until we are the last
standing, until we are the last to persist
in denial, as we are shipped off to camps

where we all are stripped, and our dark bodies lit
by the cruel light of those antique Jew-skinned
      lamps.
Decades after Dachau fell, we stand in mist
that begins and ends with ash.

3. commonly asked questions

Why are we here? What have we come to see?
What do we need to find behind the doors?
Are we searching for an apology

from the ghosts of unrepentant Nazis?
We pay the entrance fee at the front door.
Why are we here? What have we come to see?

The actors have moved on to the next scene
and set: furnace, shovel, and soot-stained door.
Are we searching for an apology

from all the Germans who refused to see
the ash falling in front of their locked doors?
Why are we here? What have we come to see

that cannot be seen in other countries?
Every country hides behind a white door.
Are we searching for an a apology

from the patient men who've hidden the keys?
Listen: a door is a door is a door.
Why are we here? What have we come to see?
Are we searching for an apology?

4. *the american indian holocaust museum*

What do we indigenous people want from our
    country?
We stand over mass graves. Our collective grief
    makes us numb.
We are waiting for the construction of our
    museum.

We too could stack the shoes of our dead and fill
    a city
to its thirteenth floor. What did you expect us to
    become?
What do we indigenous people want from our
    country?
We are waiting for the construction of our
    museum.

We are the great-grandchildren of Sand Creek
    and Wounded Knee.

We are the veterans of Indian wars. We are the
    sons
and daughters of the walking dead. We have lost
    everyone.
What do we indigenous people want from our
    country?
We stand over mass graves. Our collective grief
    makes us numb.
We are waiting for the construction of our
    museum.

5. *songs from those who love the flames*

We start the fires
on the church spire:
ash, ash.
We build tall pyres
from children's choirs:
ash, ash.
We watch flames gyre
and burn the liars:
ash, ash.

We watch flames gyre
from children's choirs:
ash ash.
We start the fires
and burn the liars:
ash, ash.

We build tall pyres
on the church spire.
ash, ash.
We build tall pyres
and burn the liars:
ash, ash.

We watch flames gyre
on the church spire:
    ash, ash.
We start the fires
from children's choirs:
ash, ash.

6. after we are free

If I were Jewish, how would I mourn the dead?
I am Spokane. I wake.

If I were Jewish, how would I remember the past?
I am Spokane. I page through the history books.

If I were Jewish, how would I find the joy to
    dance?
I am Spokane. I drop a quarter into the jukebox.

If I were Jewish, how would I find time to sing?
I am Spokane. I sit at the drum with all of my
    cousins.

If I were Jewish, how would I fall in love?
I am Spokane. I listen to an Indian woman
    whispering.

If I were Jewish, how would I feel about ash?
I am Spokane. I offer tobacco.

If I were Jewish, how would I tell the stories?
I am Spokane. I rest my hands on the podium.

If I were Jewish, how would I sleep at night?
I am Spokane. I keep the television playing until
    dawn.

If I were Jewish, how would I find my way home?
I am Spokane. I step into the river and close my
    eyes.

7. below freezing

Dachau was so cold I could see my breath
so I was thankful for my overcoat.
I have nothing new to say about death.

Each building sat at right angles to the rest.
Around each corner, I expected ghosts.
Dachau was so cold I could see my breath.

Everything was clean, history compressed
into shoes, photographs, private notes.
I have nothing new to say about death.

I wanted to weep. I wanted to rest
my weary head as the ash mixed with snow.
Dachau was so cold I could see my breath.

I am not a Jew. I was just a guest
in that theater which will never close.
I have nothing new to say about death.

I wonder which people will light fires next
and which people will soon be turned to smoke.
Dachau was so cold I could see my breath.
I have nothing new to say about death.

 *

andrei codrescu

Untitled

Soaking in rich people's tubs
Under the stars
All they want is to be kissed
And when life takes a detour
And they go slumming
The irritation is greater
Than the adventure
Peace and quiet more important
You could always buy a piece
Out there they give traffic tickets

On Drunkenness

I write my poems sober
I read them drunk
Unlike many poets
Before me who wrote
Them drunk read them drunk
And even stayed drunk
During other people's
Readings and in this
They succeeded admirably
They are mostly dead now
In poetry we call this success
After we die people read
Our poems to their sweethearts

And friends and it's a fair
Bet that they are drunk when
They do this god forbid
That they should begin
Writing their own
Drinking gets passed on
Poetry rarely
Baudelaire was right
Enivrez-vous mais
Seulement au but dâetre pisses
Pas pour la poesie
That is to say drink if you must
But don't do it for poetry please
Things are bad enough as it is

*

slam

slam

slam

* part 5

 (tracks 20–38)

About Slam Poetry

(by its founder, Marc "So What" Smith)

Slam is about all styles. It is about expanding the possibilities of poetry instead of limiting them, about injecting performance into the art of poetry, and most importantly about creating community amongst poets and audiences of diverse natures.

The competition is (or should be) secondary to the creation of enjoyable and artistically meaningful shows. Each slam evolves in its own personal way, and that's a very important characteristic of what the slam movement is—celebrating differences.

Over the years, many slam poets, including myself, have resisted the commercial exploitation of the slam. Our reasoning was that the movement belongs to thousands of people worldwide; it would be unfair for any one slam or individual to capitalize on its name and popularity. But the door to commercialization is now wide open, and we can only wait and see what it will do to the slam and performance poetry.

Slam poetry is different from many poetry movements because it is performance, and community, and audience. Many young performing poets now take it for granted that they can step up onto the stage of a club and perform their poems to one hundred, two hundred, and sometimes thousands of people. It was not that way before the slam. Even the most widely published and revered poets (the famous nobodies we called them) of the late '70s and early '80s usually read to a handful of people standing between the shelving of a bookstore or under the glaring white of fluorescent bulbs in a library. What changed that? Performance—an obligation by poets to learn the art of performing and put as much effort into that art as they did their writing. What grew from it? A worldwide community of poets who want to put the passion, excitement, and entertainment back into the presentation of poetry on stage.

The Uptown Poetry Slam at the Green Mill was an outgrowth of the Monday Night Poetry Readings and open mic at the Get Me High Lounge in Chicago begun by Ron Gillette, Joe Roarty, and myself in November 1984. At that time, poets were scoffed at if they "performed" their poems. Critics said it cheapened the art of poetry. We, the ill-bred poets of the Get Me High, did not care. Very quickly, we were attracting a larger audience than our critics believed possible. In 1985, I formed the Chicago Poetry Ensemble, which consisted of Mike Barrett, Rob Van Tyle, Jean Howard, Anna Brown, Karen Nystrom, Dave Cooper, John Sheehan, and myself. We began performing ensemble shows (the first group pieces) on a regular basis at the Get Me High and at other clubs around Chicago. We soon outgrew these small clubs and needed a larger home—more stage space and more room for our burgeoning audiences. When Dave Jemilo bought the Green Mill in the spring of 1986, I persuaded him to allow me to stage a poetry cabaret on Sundays. The Chicago Poetry Ensemble did some shows at Dave's other club, the Déjà Vu, so he was familiar with our work. On July 20, 1986, the first poetry slam show was staged. There was no competition. It was a variety show directed by myself and performed by the Chicago Poetry Ensemble. Our guest poets that night were Bob Rudnick and Mary Jo Marchnight. An open mic set began the show, peppered with ringers, audience plants, and a little music to give it more pizzazz. It was organized chaos—a three-hour train ride of supposed anarchy that was actually planned out in five-minute increments.

My initial goal was to increase the audience for poetry as a spoken art form. In the early 1980s, even the most established poets in Chicago (and probably elsewhere in the U.S.) had little or no audience when they performed public readings. The few people who did attend poetry readings were a highly specialized audience. The general public looked at poetry readings with disdain. I knew that the

public scorn for poetry readings was an outcome of how it was being presented: a lifeless monotone that droned on and on with no consideration for the structure or pacing of the event—let the words do the work, the poets would declare, mumbling to a dribble of friends, wondering why no one else had come to listen. The slam has changed that. From a handful of strangers at the Get Me High, the slam audience has grown to tens of thousands across the world.

From observing the boring poetry readings of the early 1980s, I came to understand how a better mousetrap could be made:

1. Poets were reading too many poems in open mics; an audience can stand three to five minutes of awful poetry but not fifteen; and though, on occasion, one fantastic (long-winded) poet could wow the open mic; most times it was the awful poets who would mutter on and on. So my first rule was never allow a poet to overstay his or her welcome. I encouraged the audience to boo, hiss, groan, and snap them off the stage. The present etiquette for open mic poets at the Green Mill is one or two poems and never—never!—more than five minutes.

2. Most poetry readings were one-dimensional—no surprises. By creating a show with three sets, each with its own flavor, the audience was given three opportunities to be entertained. If the open mic failed to produce anything of interest, folks could stick around to see if the guest poets in the second set would be worthwhile. If the guest poets sucked, there was always the last set and the slam competition. Turning a poetry reading into a "show" was a revolutionary idea and it worked. "Show" is the reason the slam has flourished, not competition.

3. The competition was an afterthought, it was an easy way of filling up the last half hour. Our ensemble pieces were running too short and it was an impossible feat to come up with new sketches each week. So one night we tried the competition and bingo!—everyone, even the barflies, listened. You could hear a pin drop. So we did it again the next week and thereon. Competition is a natural drama and is an exciting way of ending an evening's entertainment. Even to this day, very few of us in Chicago take the slam competition too seriously, those who do usually spin off into the land of mucky karma.

I think of the show at the Green Mill as an art form in itself. From the moment you walk in the door to the moment you're back out on the street, it's a show, and you and everything that happens are part of the action. The main character is the audience. The antagonists are the poets. The slam is organized chaos.

The structure of the National Slam is another story. It was inspired by the first Chicago slam team's trip to San Francisco in 1989 and conceived of by myself with the assistance of Chicago slam poets. The tournament, as it's known today, has been expanded and tweaked over the years, but has remained essentially the same—a four-day tournament consisting of preliminary, semi-final, and final competition nights with five judges selected from the audience—but it is always evolving. The 1990 National Slam in Chicago accommodated eight teams held in four venues. Its final night sold out the Metro Rock Club playing to 750 people—the biggest poetry event Chicago had seen for decades. It put slam on the big map. Serving more than fifty-five teams now, Nationals features events, special sideshows, meetings, arrests, love affairs…it grows and changes each year.

As any good father does, I worry about slam. Its growing success seems to threaten the eccentric nature of the art. More and more young poets copy the chops of someone they heard on a CD or saw on TV. They don't draw from their own experiences. They don't trust their own voices. I regret that the astounding variety of styles, characters, and subject matter present in the early years has, to some degree, been homogenized into a rhetorical style designed to score a "perfect 10." I also regret that many slam poets care more about building a career than they do about developing shows that offer communities, large and small, a much-needed poetic outlet.

Looking over sixteen years of slam, I still believe it provides an opportunity for outsiders and novices to get a start; it's open to all types of people. It provides a forum for performing artists to develop new works and push the envelope of their creativity. It has shown and still shows

THE ONE THAT TOASTED THEM ALL

UPTOWN POETRY SLAM

WIN

the world that the marriage of performance and poetry is a very good thing; it brings passion back into an art form that was becoming too much of an elite intellectual exercise. It has gathered an audience beyond what anyone would have thought possible. It has brought together communities of people who share a passion for creativity, words, and performance and has turned into a worldwide movement fostering free statement and a celebration of communal human spirit. It is a family of many different kinds of people who have learned to accept their differences, to argue and still be part of the family.

Slam has moved everyday people to be passionately involved with art and performance, with words and ideas, with the people who speak the words and the people who come to listen. It has given people purpose and direction. It has challenged people to examine themselves, to take chances, to get to know people and ideas they would have otherwise just passed by.

Marc Smith

Cat on a Coffin

It's you, Cat,
  Cat on the coffin
    Watching the pendulum swing,
  A paw up slapping,
  Trailing the unraveled part,
  Stalking the dead man's brains
     and finding a cold gray knot
    Looking up and out
     at the pallbearers' hearts.

It's you, Cat,
  Cat felis catus catus
    Scrounging near the twilight
     for the already dead,
    Claiming the troth
     of the undertaken souls
  While the weeping acidic rain
    Taps hats forever.

It's you, amoral children,
    Suppressing your fantastic fears,
    Bending to peer inside the shiny box
     Where a ludicrous shape
    Begins to arise—

The cat-head winks.
   Eyes grow wide.
  Lips shout faceless,
    "Be mine! Be mine!"

It's you, Doctor Spade,
  Slipping your wiry brown fingernail
    down the hip of her jeans,
Poking and dragging the egg yolk out.
Tomorrow's baby, a grappled breakfast.

It's you, cocaine fool,
Sniff-snortin' to feel so good
  about so damn little
  when you got so much,
Just wishin' your nostrils
  were stainless steel
And your mind
  a Pillsbury cake.
It's you, mid-morning American jogger,
  wearing the shelves of J C Penney's
Like the stripes of your flag.

It's you, bike-outlaw,
Smelling of pig grease, Quaker State,
  and Gulf Supreme,
Tattooing the buttocks of JoJo's little sister,
Head-giver whenever you please.

It's you, old veteran at the VFW Hall,
  wrapping your loose lips around
    another smudged glass of gin,
Bemoaning Tommy Dorsey's demise,
Foaming up a bromide lyric
Before your bowed head
    makes a wrinkle on the rail.

It's you, subscribers to a thousand magazines.
  And you,
    the writers for a thousand magazines.
And you,
    the publishers of anything that sells.
And you, the buyers of little children
  On super-eight film   video-cassettes
    Color!   Sound!
It's you, hot-tubbers,
  Finding it easier to suck
    in the rush of a whirlpool
Than to speak
  after the pleasure has passed.

It's you, Pink Hands   Pink Face   White Ass,
  Screaming and stomping your feet.
  The Old Blues Picker in the red silk shirt
    taps his long
                  flat
                    toe
  And you want to screammmmmmmm
    him out of his addiction
  But he just closes
                          his
                    narcotic
          eyes.

It's you, nigger,
  Bein' nigger,
Callin' the nigger downstairs
"NIGGER!"
While you poke your nigger
  Roscoe, to his bride.

It's you, actress
  With the commercial hair, com-
Mercial lips, commercial skin, commer-
  Cial smile, commercial sin
  Cerity.

It's you, Cowboy-Sailor-Skier,
Player of football, basketball,
  Tennis, baseball, hockey.

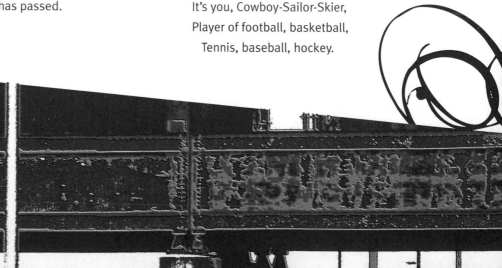

It's you, up there on the sixty-ninth floor,
Drinking Chateau Au Briand
  From a newspaper thin glass,
  Listening to Rachmaninoff,
  Waiting for some Chicano sister
To come lick your Chopin.

It's you, Pork Chop
  firing your twenty-two caliber pistol
    at the front porch family
  from your buddy's beat-up wagon,

avenging some asshole cousin's outrage
  over a dead dog bludgeoned
by a blackjack pulled
  from his sister's purse.

It's you, clowny politician
cultivating your crawl space
  with the humus of little boys,
  while bouncing aerobic dancers
fry Friday nights by the ounce
dreaming of the morning
  when the dance will be over
and the feeding
Can 1 2 3 next begin!

It's you, disco partners,
  counterpointing the wiggles of your hips
in unison with a world that marvels
  at such profound rhythms.

It's you, pumping iron in the basement,
  preparing for the fifteenth year
when your Daddy upstairs
  will no longer pump
your mother's face
  bloody.

It's you shop-lifted children,
  Taken away to be sodomized slowly
And then slaughtered on the silver screen.

It's you, all of you,
  Divided and sub-divided,
  divided again
  Split into units
  smaller
Than the smallest
  pronoun.

  It's you
  The cat has dragged you in.
He'll feast on you tomorrow.
The Cat, the hardcase cat,
  Cat on the Coffin.

You're string between his teeth.

*

The Father Has Faded
a gambling rogation

The Father has faded.

What he waaassssss   crapped out.
Now under the alters
The deacons roll   the no come line,
Smackin' the cubes   against the green cloth rood,
Bettin' that there ain't no salvation.
    The Father has faded

And the Player's head has fallen.
The last whispers   off his promise-to lips,
The faint vespers   in his glory-be eyes,
The could-be points of paradise
As lastly he looked up
Are gone.
    The Player's head has fallen.

And the Word is spoken. Knocks on wood.
Lets Evil in through the backdoor
Where Daddy Joe Crow prayin' "Hard four!"   "No
    four!"
Cops the action
In the blue smoke light   of a hidden sanctuary.
    The Word is spoken,

And while all the neighborhood boys
Are dealin' down their darkness...
    Oblivious to who?

While all the neighborhood boys
Are dealin' down their darkness,
    The A Number One Kingpin
    Comes hoppin' off a boxcar.

Now, has he come back maybe
Judgment Day
To double-cross the Daddy?
Has he come back snappin'
Like a rooster rappin'
    "Find me!
    You honey-come-eleven!"

Has he come back blowin'
"Papa knows! Papa knows!
    Papa knows
    You throw sevens every time!"

Has he come back maybe?

Preacher smiles. Evil grins.
The rack pulls in the dice.
A loaded pair drops.
Now the Kingdom's got to come
On Phoney Bones!
    "TOSS THE DICE, DADDY!"

"Father! Father! FATHER!"
You know, we all need somethin'. You know
Half the time we don't know what we're doin'.
You know,
There are a million of us doubtful characters
Drifting in the shadow patched sunlight
    of a fragmented sky.
Father! Don't forget us! Don't let us go.
Don't forget ... Joe. "Little Joe.
    Little Joe!   LITTLE JOE!"

The Word is spoken,
And the Spirit flies.
A long finger comes out of the clouds, Smoothes
    an ash into the green felt.
"A miracle!"   "The hard way!"
"Double deuce!" cries the Crow
Scratchin' up the dollars,
Stuffin' 'em in his pants.

Then Evil shouts, "Cops at the corner.
    Run!"
Fast blades cut the shadows.
Blood pools on the green floor
    Lightning!   Black alley dust!
    Vanishing moon!

Preacher scats in a blues beat rush.
Two, three boxcars roll away in red.
Father hangs in the doorway
    and death coughs up his blood.

Quickly, the Preacher grabs a passing ladder
Climbs a few rungs.
Sighs at the engine's tune
    hummin'
"Snake eyes   snake eyeeeeesssssssss."

The Father has faded.

*

Dusty Blues

The moon, when swinging trumpets blow,
Goes blue as red the rhythm cuts
The rain with saucy cinder-beats;
And blackbirds hop the high hot lines.

   (It's a scats madder scene.)

In cellar grays where notes collide
The bulb's half eclipse cleaves a brain;
And "Death," the wailing madman cries,
"Leaves me half breaths, baby."

Oh, the wind that crosses elms at night
Flows through the tubes of tacit life
Proclaiming in its haunting moan,
"All is senseless, Pops."

But the brew within the brassy stove
Cooks clean to alabaster bones;
And "Fame" the jiving jazzman's told,
"Hangs with the blackbirds
Up on those high hot lines!"

   It's a blue-black crooked dream.

*

Street Musician

A musician stands out on a street corner
And begins to play
Melodies melodies up through the leaves
Like a big cat climbin'
Melodies.
Testin' each branch higher.
Reachin' out a black paw
To catch a note
High in the tree.
Melody.

The musician blows his horn
And makes an air of blue scarf
Swirl out of the bell...
Floats into the street light
Like a sheen of lonely attitudes—
One voice
High in the tree.
It's that melody.

Now, this musician...you can call him Cat,
Cat Blow the Horn's Hymn Blue
Pullin' the brim down on a blue hat
Playin' things as they are muted—
A little sound caught in his throat;
Mutated—
Things as they are with a difference,
A difference in everything he does.

Oh this Cat, Cat Blow the Horn's Hymn Blue,
Wearin' the blue hat,
Blue hat things as they are,
Blue lips playin' as you hear them now —
Rips through the creamy moon and the midnight
A sound that says,
    "It's love.
It's love that's tearin' him apart."

Oh, he's just a guy,
A guy out on the lonely street corner
Wishin' that he could press
To the woman in the window light
The music he would play
If he could catch her
In that impossible note.

Play her like Saturn Ring Swing Around Hazy
    Mars.
Play her at the window three flats up
Moonlight, lake wind, trees in the courtyard
    swayin',
Potted plants green, summer screens,
Faces of Coltrane, Brown, and Adderley
Mixin' in the sounds of the night
With his own heart rhythms.

Oh, this guy, like a big cat climbin'
On a stone ledge walkin'
Thinks. He thinks
That if he could just move his hands
Up from the bottoms of her feet,
Caress her belly,
Kiss her 'til she died.
A blue fire spinnin' from his head blown out.
A flame in his tongue freezin' her
In a measure of time that won't let loose.

He thinks
This is the holler. This is the moan.
This is the only note I cannot find alone.
So take it. Take from me the creamy moon,
The crazy wind, the midnight.
Take all there is and all there's gonna be.
Take all there is and all there's gonna be.
...and so one morning she did.
And in the yellow morning light he found.
Her blue lips parted on his belly cold.
Blue lights spinnin' in a sky burnt out.
A flame wick in the tree tops gone cool.

*

track 46

Pull the Next One Up

When you get to the top of the mountain
Pull the next one up.
Then there'll be two of you
Roped together at the waist
Tired and proud, knowing the mountain,
Knowing the human force it took
To bring both of you there.

And when the second one has finished
Taking in the view,
Satisfied by the heat and perspiration under the
    wool,

Let her pull the next one up;
Man or woman, climber of mountains.
Pull the next hand over
The last jagged rock
To become three.
Two showing what they've already seen.
And one knowing now the well-being with being
Finished with one mountain,
With being able to look out a long way
Toward other mountains.
Feeling a temptation to claim victory
As if mountains were human toys to own.

When you ask how high is this mountain
With a compulsion to know
Where you stand in relationship to other peaks,
Look down to wherefrom you came up
And see the rope that's tied to your waist
Tied to the next man's waist,
Tied to the next woman's waist,
Tied to the first man's waist,
To first woman's waist
...and pull the rope!

Never mind the flags you **see** flapping on
    conquered pinnacles.
Don't waste time scratching inscriptions into the
    monolith.
You are the stone itself.
And each man, each woman up the mountain,
Each breath exhaled at the peak,
Each glad-I-made-it ... here's-my-hand,
Each heartbeat wrapped around the hot skin
of the sun-bright sky,
Each noise panted or cracked with laughter,
Each embrace, each cloud that holds everyone
in momentary doubt...

All these are inscriptions of a human force that
    can
Conquer conquering hand over hand pulling the
    rope
Next man up, next woman up.
Sharing a place, sharing a vision.
Room enough for all on all the mountain peaks.
Force enough for all

To hold all the hanging bodies
Dangling in the deep recesses of the mountain's
    belly
Steady...until they have the courage...
Until they know the courage...
Until they understand
That the only courage there is is
To pull the next man up
Pull the next woman up
Pull the next up...Up...Up.

The Poetry Scene:
no one way
(by Marvin Bell)

In the 1980s, there came a rebirth of coffeehouse readings, thanks in part to the invention of the poetry slam in 1986 by Marc Smith. Sunday nights, Smith took over the Green Mill Jazz Lounge in Chicago for a rough-and-ready contest among poets. When I first went to see the show at the Green Mill, I imagined the slam might be either a coffeehouse on speed or a tavern on decaf. I have witnessed my share of coffeehouse readings: the good, the bad, and the ugly, but mostly the limp, the stiff, and the dull.

I still held to Whitman's notion of a great audience for poetry, which meant an audience far beyond the classroom. But readings, even as they had proliferated on college campuses, hadn't enlarged the audience. This was different. By the time the official Slam competition got underway that evening, whoever had happened upon the scene, even if intending just to peek, had been drawn into it. The crowd was eager and alert. This wasn't the laid-back coffeehouse of the '50s and '60s. Nor was it the tense faux-macabre meeting of some Dead Poets Society. It was for fun and fiction, for truth and drama, for song and thought, and all of it for everyone. I thought the poems were quite good that night. They had been written to be heard aloud rather than lingered over on the page, but many of them would have done fine on the page too.

The character of the Chicago slam owed much to the informal brilliance of its host and founder, Marc Smith. It was lively, it was fun, and Smith had just the right mixture of poetry, wit, and good nature to make it happen. He mixed humor and generosity with a sense of high quality. He made reference to other poets and poems. He was receptive to poetry on all levels and responsive to the best of it, and his language and manner taught the audience to do the same. To quote from Jack Kerouac about The Subterraneans, it was "hip but not slick, cool but not corny." When I think of early critics dismissing the poetry slam, I see Smith reciting a poem by Wallace Stevens. It was a poem as much of the page as of the air, but somehow he spoke the poem so that it was immediate and accessible from the very start.

And then he kept going, reciting, building on the Stevens poem, and the poetry he was reciting was still fascinating, having evolved seamlessly right out of the Stevens. Marc had written his own poem, using Stevens at the beginning and end. And the longer poem was a kind of comment on the shorter poem. It used it, enlarged it, applied it. Out of a poem for books, used perhaps in some classroom for rote memorization, Marc Smith had made a poem for recitation. Marc's presentation was virtuoso—both the writing and the reading of it—and for me, it stood for the very nature of this developing phenomenon that came to be known worldwide as the poetry slam. That is, the slam would be poetry, not ideas about poetry, and it would be poetry in motion and poetry in action, not fixed to a pedestal, and it would validate the lowbrow and the highbrow at the same time. Perhaps, after all, Walt Whitman was watching and truly, now, poets had begun coming out of the woodwork.

In the '90s, poetry slams spread throughout the country and abroad. Poetry had an audience in coffeehouses again, in bars, on city stages, and, as always, in the academy. Meanwhile, graduate writing programs sprang up everywhere, it seemed, because young people wanted and needed them. With new sources of private and public support, however pitiful our government's support for the arts compared to the rest of the developed world, reading programs proliferated, anthologies seemed to reproduce themselves, literary magazines that would formerly have perished in one or two years stayed afloat, publishers organized contests to help them select poetry books from among the thousands of manuscripts sent to them, independent publishers won a larger readership, there came an outpouring of videos and CDs and 'zines, and young and old alike found new paths to poetry.

Poetry in America now has a huge cultural presence, with many venues, many roles, and its own official month. There are the literary poets, those who push the technical envelope, who have a larger audience than they once had, but whose

home

remains the university and the publishing houses. There are the coffeehouse poets, the street poets, and the poetry slam poets, who bring the energy of the performer to poetry aloud. There are "poetry-in-the-schools" programs and the urban after-school soccer and poetry program for eight-to-twelve-year-olds known as "America Scores." There are thousands of graduate students enrolled in MFA programs and low-residency writing programs. There are summer writing conferences from coast to coast, and abroad in places like Prague, Paris, and St. Petersburg. There are programs with names like "ArtsShare" that send poets to perform in the community. Most states now have poet laureates. One former president and one senator who ran for president have published books of poetry, as have well-known actors and athletes. There was a period when judges were writing their lighter verdicts in doggerel. Even radio and TV occasionally make a place for poetry apart from local access.

Much of this poetry is just wordplay or heartfelt writing that feels the emotional spirit of poetry. Poetry, like water, seeks its own level. But there has also been a great outpouring of the kind of poetry that one wants to, or needs to, reread or rehear, the poetry that embodies the emotional complexity of life. There is no one way to write and no right way to write. If the poets of academic achievement and the poets of the poetry slam still largely dismiss one another, well, poetry is a big tree and not all the branches can be expected to touch. The poet and publisher Jonathan Williams once said, "The trouble with American poets is that they want everyone else to write like them, but not as well."

Poetry is a great big Yes. Yes to formalists, yes to free verse writers, yes to surrealists, yes to political poets, yes to the poets of wordplay and slippery self-consciousness, yes to the Dadaists, yes to the mystics, yes to the scholar-poets, yes to the punsters, yes to the anti-poetic poets, yes to the prose-poets, yes to the poets who write about a word and to those who write about a people, yes to the poets who write about a blade of grass and to those who write about a war. It isn't about the books and the prizes often reserved for those of us who feel the charge to push the envelope. It isn't about someone's top ten or first hundred. It's about body and soul, time and eternity, life and death. The imagination is not a luxury or a college elective. It is, more than ever, a survival skill.

regie gibson

prayer

for the drummers hands
severed before they could strike skin

for the seventh string of unplayed guitars
gone suicidal with longing

for the fifth tendon of the hobbled upright

the fourth key of discarded trumpets
tortured into silent confession

for the ghostly gray keys of murdered pianos
condemned to inhabit the cadavers of their
    killers

prayer for every dancers legs
stolen and pawned

for all poets made to eat their tongues

the artists eyes

painted shut by the color blind
the singers throat made mausoleum
of infant hymns

this elegy is for your aborted souls

your mahabarata suffocated while dreaming of
    birth

your music massacred while praying

your song assassinated in flight

for you whose flames
could have scorched

open paths between us
and ourselves

and for us
condemned to never know it

*

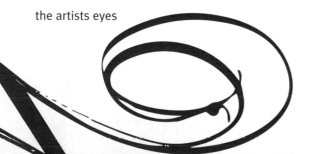

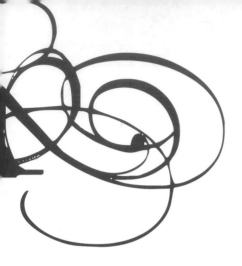

track 38

it's a teenage thang
(for every teenager who has rebelled against their parents by sneekin out to party)

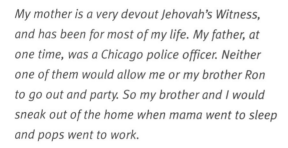

My mother is a very devout Jehovah's Witness, and has been for most of my life. My father, at one time, was a Chicago police officer. Neither one of them would allow me or my brother Ron to go out and party. So my brother and I would sneak out of the home when mama went to sleep and pops went to work.

We would take the CTA (Chicago Transit Authority) east to Halsted Street or the Madison bus west to the "Factory" or the North Ave to DaVinci Manor to get our groove on while listening to house music. Inside those parties we found a new communion with others and ourselves. This is a late recollection of what it meant to be young, defiant, and feeling your oats at sixteen.

—Regie Gibson

bass slides in on all fours
rabid with feral look in eyes
bodies   twist
            into
        blasphemous
        angle of
    rebellion/defiance

somethin smellin
like
                    jail time
cuts across air
                    like hand fulls of zirconia
scratchin shit
            out of plexiglass sky

over in corner
                cue balls psychotic   smack
breaks up tribe of stripes and solids
on field of green

black eight sinks
thru smoky haze of aw shits
damns as ten spots reluctantly
ruffle they ways
out pissed off pockets

d.j. priest
sittin reverently in the pulpit
jacks sounds in alternatin patterns
of thirty three and thirds

spinnin gospel
of our faith
as congregations hands

reach heavenward
exposin our palm to angles

as we hope to catch a
hallowed high five
from a god whose
pissed cuz shes gotta work
the night shift

tonight

we be young
virile   sweatin passions
ya gotta experience to understand

we don't give a damn
bout tympanic
cartilaginous erosion
of inner ears

weakened by 1200 to many
hot grindin weekends
of buttbumpinwoofinandtweetin

we don't give a damn
bout ass kickin
waitin on us when we get
home way past curfew

(ok a little)

but tonight we only care bout
ass kickin bass and drum
can give

ass kickin bass and drum
can heal

tonight we live for strobelights
kissin vision
bringin new sight

for floors moanin with
weight of young
flippant attitudes

glasses mumblin
speech of stolen
kisses

sky explodin with funk
of flirtin smiles

we live for bodega crew
comin up from barrio

bringin supple
brown morenas con
hips like congas
gon-boppin
6/8 rhythm
from front door to dance floor

got you tryin to speak in language
you aint never tongued before
uh   mira maimi   uh   pasie aqee po oon
momentato po fayvo
(or somethin like that)

big   red   manzana lips
partin ever so slightly
revealin thin sliver of pink tongue
rollin like scarlet smoke off roof of latina mouths

we live for sisters
blue blacks   honey browns
heavenly ebonies   gettin down
on legs shaped like mamas soulfood
with a whole lotta attitude

calves

carved

outta hams and hocks

with backsides big   round   sweet   and tender
as grandmamas homemade biscuits
(have mercy)

they hair icked
slicked
tricked
or picked out
into
asymmetricalisoscelesrhomboidparallelograms

and a few other forms
defying geometric
classification

tonight

we be young   virile
sweaty with passion
you gotta experience to understand

tonight

be our night to hold somebodies body
to feel they eye lashes brush up against
face on slow jam

feel thin wispy fingers
of they breath invade
sensitive conch shell ear
like well trained guerillas

to hold them close firm heavin nubile
against the mask of teenage knowin
and adolescent pretence

somethin deep inside us
that useta paint on caves
realizes this moment contains
    a forever
and eternal memories be born
    one forever at a time

    tonight

we be young   virile   sweaty with passions
you gotta
    understand to experience

and tonight we dont care or give a damn
why our parents dont seem to understand

why sweat   be friend of ours
and tonight we gots to get real real
    friendly

*

in the year i loved your mother
for my daughter safiya who needs to know this

in the year i loved your mother
i lived a glorious death
i was satellite traveling between blood and star
a planet evolving through rage and grief

in the year i loved your mother
was a time of drought and deluge
a season of rain and ruin

between us much soil and water
an illiterate ocean of language and diction

i arrived to her half broken half breaking

in the year i loved your mother
we were drum and drone
a volley of polemic and ideal

once i glimpsed you
waving at me from her mouth
as dawn met our shoulders
she whispered your name

we became the thin line
between sea and mountain
valley and sky

in the year i loved your mother
gravity abandoned me to her
she was vortex—a black hole
sewn into the belly of a continent
crushing all into singularity.

grapewaswinewas
soundwassongwas
motionwasdancewas
dovewasvulturecirclingwaslandingwas
all that was : was herYYY

the year i loved your mother
was the year tragedy tamed tongues

we severed ours   stitched them into
one anothers mouths we grew fluent
in speaking pain.

we brought stones from our pockets
traded them hurled them back towards
each others wounds   and those that missed
were gathered later   were used to build our walls

she was an equinox of razors when i found her
an autumn of featherless wings
caught in this gale of a man

your mother was: soft lips cutting calluses
from my knuckles

a silk fist logged hard in my mouth
where it opened into a sunflower
widening in the crag of my throat

in her skin i was cryptic blasphemy
transparent   decoded   holy

*

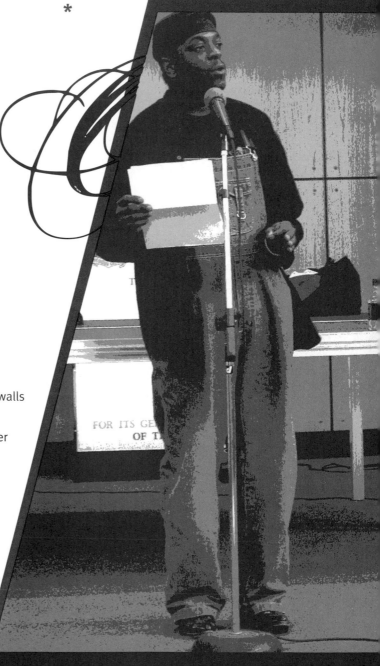

Once a "virgin, virgin, virgin" at the Green Mill

(by Dr. Richard Prince)

I first came to the Uptown Poetry Slam at the Green Mill on a wintry Sunday in January 1988, and have been coming back ever since; I believe I hold the record for attending more Poetry Slams at the Green Mill than anyone save Marc Smith himself. Sometimes people ask me why I have kept coming back week after week for fourteen years: I keep coming back because for me the Poetry Slam has not lost its magic or its appeal.

The Poetry Slam experience for me starts at the Green Mill and the particular excitement the club generates. First of all, there is the Green Mill itself; it takes a lot of its current character from its owner Dave Jemilo—a tough no-nonsense guy who could have come right out of a Raymond Chandler story. The way Jemilo runs the bar in this former Al Capone speakeasy, what could be more Chicago?

I love the wide sweep of Broadway as it goes south from Lawrence toward the El tracks, the Aragon, the Riviera, the Uptown Theater, the great old art-deco post office, and the People's Church. Just a couple of blocks to the north is the wonderment of New Chinatown on Argyle Street: Uptown has a history of being a point of entry for immigrants, including Native Americans, hillbillies, people who live in SROs, and now huge numbers of Asians. There's a great greasy Mexican restaurant where young Mexican guys take their families to eat (always a good sign for a restaurant!) right up the street from the Mill. And then there are people on the street—homeless beggars, kids going to the shows at the Aragon or the Riv, cabdrivers, people coming home from work (yes, even on Sundays!) trying to catch the bus. In the summer, you can see people going to and from the lake, and in the winter, there is that sharp Chicago wind coming off Lake Michigan that all Chicago natives regard with awe and respect. This Uptown/Green Mill Chicago is the Chicago I find in Nelson Algren, Studs Terkel, Mike Royko, Richard Wright, Saul Bellow, and way back to Sandburg and Dreiser and Farrell.

As powerful as the vibe in the street reverberates inside the bar, there is no getting past the remarkable character and founder of slam poetry, the Chicago guy, Marc Smith. In many ways he encapsulates the mood of the neighborhood, the ambience of the bar, and the voices of all the great Chicago writers. To this day, I am continually drawn to his shows week after week to hear the heart and soul of what it means for many people to live and work in Chicago.

Also, Marc's unique beliefs about "reading" poetry and his beliefs about what poetry should mean and does have helped forge the Slam experience. There has always been a mood or a tone in the bar itself that Marc works hard to create—namely that anyone who comes in is welcome: before the show he greets new people and introduces them to people he knows. The audience is always part of the show, so that when he and anyone else is on stage, there is this open and implied connection between poet and audience: there is often a very receptive mood in the crowd that enables the poet, who is often nervous about getting up in front of two hundred strangers, to bare his or her soul! This can be very inspiring, and I have seen many poets feed off an audience to not only write more and write better, but to read or perform their poetry to an audience that is hungry for a good or new poem. Patricia Smith is the poet who comes to mind as someone who flourished this way. There is another side to this, however: when a bad poet performs—that is, when a poseur, or someone who is maudlin or sentimental, or someone who thinks a bad stand-up comedy routine is poetry, or someone who doesn't know when to stop, or someone who may be drunk (not surprising in a bar on a Sunday night!)—when one of these people tries to perform, the audience will usually let these folks know exactly what they think with groans and hisses.

This audience involvement was one of the things I love about Marc Smith's Uptown Poetry Slam: I love the closeness of poet and audience as anyone could go up to a poet and talk to him or her right there on the spot. I also like the idea that poets have a special directness to their audience—they had the idea that they

were speaking to real people who would react to what they say, the relationship was more than just pen to page: these were words and images and rhythms meant to be experienced in the ways poetry must have been before books and schools came.

I have never thought of slam poetry or performance poetry as being brand new or something invented by Marc Smith or Bob Holman or any of these other poets and performers who are all over the slam scene. The people whom I have seen perform are part of the old bardic or folk tradition of people gathering to sing, tell stories, and share with words what they think and feel. This tradition encompasses the Homeric epic, medieval ballads, the English broadside, and any culture's folk songs and folk-tales. And then beyond that was my own experience as a teacher and a scholar of American poetry, and my own sense of how important Walt Whitman was and is to American literature. When I came to the Green Mill that first night, I remember feeling exhilarated by some of the poets on stage and saying to my friend that old familiar refrain from Whitman, "I hear America singing—its varied carols I hear."

In the weeks and years following those initial experiences at the Green Mill, I have found that poets who read or perform their poetry expose themselves in good and bad ways. I have been to countless "academic poetry" readings at colleges, universities, bookstores, churches, and libraries. But I think the poetry reading that left the biggest impression on me was when I had the chance to hear Robert Frost read at Orchestra Hall shortly before his death. This was right after he had read "The Gift Outright" at President Kennedy's inauguration in 1961, which was probably one of the high points in his very rich and long life. Later on, I came to realize that Robert Frost was probably the twentieth century's greatest U.S. performance poet. Throughout his career, he traveled all over the country giving public performances; he must have thought that his poetry did not belong only bound up in books and manuscripts.

Upon first hearing poetry at the Green Mill, I was reminded of this, and I thought, "Am I going to hear the next Robert Frost or Walt Whitman at one of these poetry slams? Isn't this what a lot of poets do or should do? Poetry has many more dimensions than simply words on the page! What do poems sound like?" The sound of the words, the rhythms of the lines, the tone of images, and all the other things that the performers can bring to their words is the very essence of poetry—especially in the tradition of Whitman and Frost. And as long as Whitman and Frost are dead and gone, where can people who love poetry go for this kind of experience? When I go to the Green Mill, I can hear this in slam poetry!

Low Down in the Get Me High Lounge

Rustling slop bucket
Of fluid jazz.
Sweaty enclosure
A be-bop rag.
Enclave in
Blue-collar 'hood.
Merged through
Her twisted
Flugelhorn tube:
Lagos to Jamestown
Via human trade
Riffs torn
From arms
In holy raids.
B-flat scraping
Eroded stage
Peeling words
Off the poet's wall.
Plastered strata of
Talmudic scrawl.
Graffiti—
Bare and unrevealing
Seeping from the

Jazz-soaked ceiling.
Resistance to the
Tar-filled air
Blue-note time
Suspended there.
Bassman slide on
Yo' dirty G string
Meandering down
Make that thang
Sang.

*

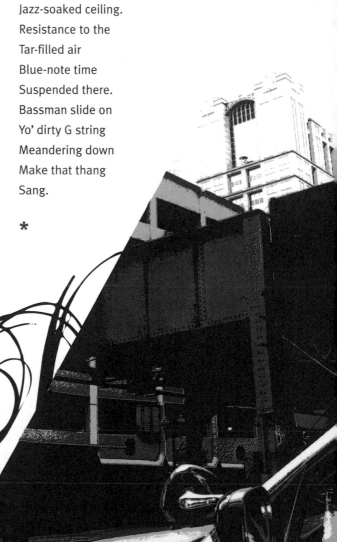

The Ice Worm

You can take away that net.
I'm not much of a performer,
one of those that struts and shines,
delivering my personal angst
in easy technicolor rhymes.
I'm from the old school
where poets named things, told the truth—
the hard truths nobody wanted to hear.
When they created beauty,
by God, people were stunned.
When they failed,
they took the fall.

Truth, beauty, the arcane lore,
what are they against *People* magazine,
USA Today, CNN, and a lying president?
Mass production, the glory and the curse of the
    20th century,
replays words, pictures, politics, and bad art
until it all seeps in like an Eskimo winter,
and sometimes the only way to clear the
    synapses
is a vigorous cranial wallbanger—or a good
    poem.
So let me tell you something I remember.
Maybe you've seen it, too.

At four or five years old,
when I was starting to lose my imagination,
had stopped coloring dogs' tongues orange and
    cats' feet purple,
I must have been home from school sick
and bored with staying inside the lines,
when I saw something where nothing should
    have been.

Atop a bare sycamore branch
where the sun should have melted it away,
a piece of ice moved.
It humped itself up like an inchworm
and moved along,
humped and moved,
humped and moved.
When it got to the end of the branch,
its head searched and couldn't find anywhere to
    go,
so it humped off the end of the branch and fell
with a couple of tumbling flashes into a
    snowbank below.

Once I saw one, I saw more.
They were on trees, the snow and the sidewalks.
As my chest and throat and head
were about to burst with excitement,
my mother came up behind me.
She saw what I saw,
and light flashed in her warm brown eyes
the way it had off the ice worm.
She opened the window and slid her finger
under one on the window sill.
I watched it inch along.
Before it got to the end,
I picked it up,
and all I felt was dampness
between my thumb and forefinger.

I haven't seen an ice worm in years.
I'm not sure what that means, except for this—
there ought to be things that we can't see easily,
that TV networks, magazines, companies,
and the goddamned politicians can't use,
small, beautiful things that disappear
as soon as we get our hands on them.

*

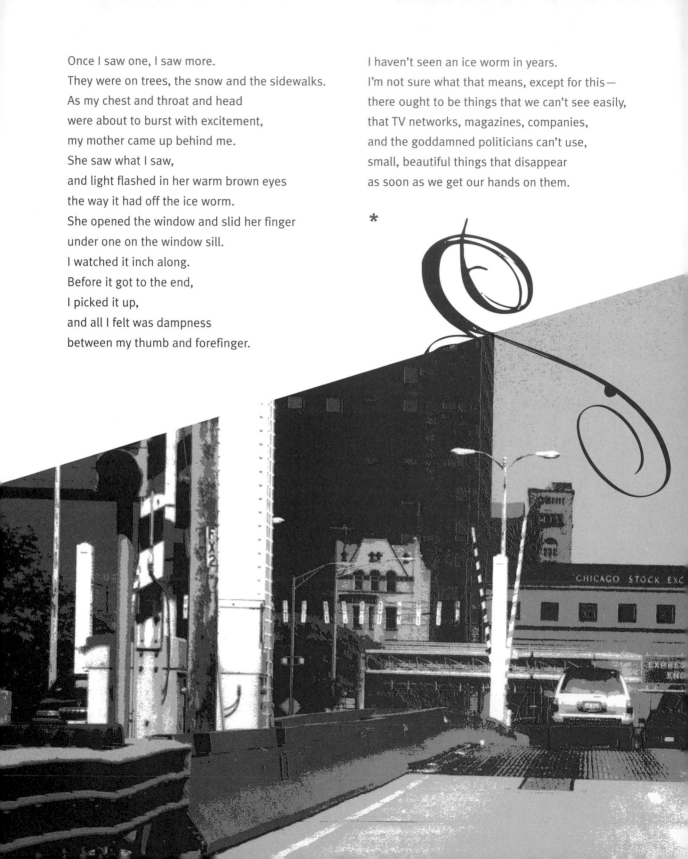

brenda moossy

*hear...

track 36

What I Said to the Man Installing the Hot Tub

When the man came to install my hot tub,
I said, "It must be in a clearing, Mister,
'cause I want to see the stars!"

No matter that I am in full view
of my neighbor's junked cars and defunct
    appliances and that it is their custom to spill
tumbling thru the screen door.
Wooden frame slaps against the jamb.
The man (He's the boyfriend) stands legs apart
    for balance against the shifting ground.
His shirt, ripped and open, the tails
flap in disbelief. The women,
mother and daughter, are drunken sentries:
boulders blocking the door. They spit.
They bellow. "Get outta here!"
"Get the fuck outta here!"
It's no matter to them that he wails,

fists clenched,
arms pleading
"But, she needs a man!
SHE NEEDS A MAN!!"
And I think, Who? Who is that boy
referring to? Don't he know?
We are all in need of comfort here.

I want to see the stars, I say.
I need to see the stars.

And it's no matter that in the dark,
I am an Earth-bound moon.
Naked and round, I skim along the grass,
walk to roll, into a steaming sea with a hisssss...
But, you see that spark
from my neighbor's cigarette yonder?
Lord, it stings like shame.

And no matter that in mid-life,
I carry my childhood fear of the dark
up-close, near my heart—a troublesome babe
I can never be free from.
In the dark, I court logic:
I name the levels of the atmosphere,
chart the configuration of stars. Hell,
I even analyze the chemical composition
of astral dust. But it don't matter.
The voice inside my head still whispers:
"what if...
they's monsters?"
"what if...
I shut my eyes, a crazyman comes and
slits my throat?"
"What if...
I stare at the heavens and the sky cracks wide?"
Angels could slip through in the blinding.
Stars rip from the firmament
form letters words prophecies of light
No matter
No matter
I will watch for the miracles to fall.

I want to see the stars, Mister.
I got to see the stars.

*

Michael Kadela

michael kadela

xxx

the stone wagers its time to the wind
and another prophecy bemoans of the night
and were clouds to have been harvesting
strict bows of sleet, of muck, of rain

the earth of more bccarthing grain
should probably rise
and describe to smile

yet hasn't there been at least one dusk
that was paved with gray
and then dragged for awhile?

so good evening, evening
please meet my good friend, afternoon
she is rather lovely (or has been so)
and I believe that you would have beautiful
    children
the two of you, between
during whom shall I mainly think
of many things, notwithstanding
a certain moon, or somewhat sky
but also this

for there is one certain little look which sings
the undoing of the lesser years
and when the little ones grow into night
I hope they remember their happy conception
because I love You is a big place, filled

now, spring may argue, I love You is spring
but spring is not so big a place
as is big a place
as is I love You is
and spring,
though filled quite completely
is filled quite completely
only
with spring

I love You is a summer and a deathbed and a
    pencil
it is a big place, filled
with Laundromats and asthma attacks
and tapeworm waltzes
and other strange dances

that explain not a thing
to the curious watchers

except that there is room to spare for those
    inclined to dance

it is a big place
filled with seven springs and three tornadoes
and toast and eggs and
battleships
that lack the range
to fire outside
so widest it

I love You is a steeple wish
I love You is a pound of flesh
I love You is a lighter foot
a box of walks
a fishing net
an albatross
a callused heel
a bird of clay
a birthday cake

I love You is a big place filled with Awake

LXXIV

there are ten thousand forfeit heartbeats
I have placed aside
for safekeeping

just in case you change your mind
and if by that the sun were then to rise
with meaning
I might take them out
and sweetly suffer them
to sight
and breath
with you

by my forfeit hearts which beat I swear this true
that you
that you, you are a blood
that runs
so and swiftly through
my what and ever what
my ever
my
my what
my every my is you

there are palaces wherein there I have wept
where I have wondered of your lips
where I have crept upon the dirty floors of if
and licked the bruises of my knees there into
    peaches

into paradigms

I do not give one single shit
for anything less
than my happiest thought

a truer me to see me through
sees this:

your eyes are closed
and you love me

*

steve marsh

Belated Valentine:
A Work in Progress

I woke this morning with that shadow feeling I'd
    been dreaming
significant dreams—
Strong and powerful,
Richly full of meaning.
But I was unable to recall them no matter how
    hard I tried.
Chasing them only makes it worse,
Like groping for the other tennis shoe
Lost under the bed
Just beyond my reach,
Closing my hand on something,
To discover it is only
So much dust and dog hair.

I closed my eyes,
Breathed deeply,
And reached for that familiar place.

But the Universe asked me a question.
Why do I continue to love you?

And I begin to answer immediately because
Confidence is the feeling we have before we
    understand the situation.

Why in the face of all we have seen,
and failed to see in each other,
Do we persevere?

I begin to understand it is a matter of pride.
And, pride is, after all,
what we have.
Vanity is what others have.

So, in pride or vanity I offer:
I love you because I have always loved you.

And the Universe knows this is not a whole truth.
It knows it like it knows we can't pray a lie.

I try again.
I love you because of all we have been through
    together.

And the Universe does not like this cliché any
    better.
It asks, with all the Aristotelian logic it can
    muster,
Do you not manifest "all that you have been
    though together?"
The Universe knows and will not let me get away
    with half a truth.
We have been through "all that"
Because we have put each other through "all
    that."

It asks another question:
How can you assert love after all you have seen?

The helplessness after surgeries;
The weakness in the face of adversity;
The cowardice in the face of confrontation;
Weight gain,
Hair loss,
Reduced libido,
Nakedness at forty,
Nakedness at fifty?
The knowledge that the final solution does not
    involve Bean-o.

And I begin, in answer, to list the qualities I
    admire in you:
Tolerance,
Patience,
Trust,
Faithfulness.
Forgiveness.

But the Universe will not allow this equivocation
    either.
And because the Universe is a big believer in the
    Socratic Method,
it asks
Why do I love my dog?

I confess to perceiving a similar list.

The Universe sends me the spring songbirds
    early,
Who sing, and feed,
who show me community in bright colors
And high energy.
The birds know nothing of our sorrow.

And the Universe asks again,
In the face of this sorrow, why do I continue to
    love you?

It is not because Mothers are better than Fathers.
It is not because women are better than men.
It is not because teaching is better than poetry.
It is not because daughters are better than
    husbands.

And slowly, the answer,
Or rather the understanding that there is no
    answer,
Begins to reveal itself to me.

There is no aetiology for love.

I do not love you because
I do not love you in spite of
I do not love you since
I do not love you in so much as
I do not love you for the reason that

There is no reason,
No logic,
No syllogistic proof.
It simply is.
I love you.
It comes about without cause
And with luck it is returned
without cause.

That is why love fits more aptly into poetry than
    paint.
It is not revealed to the mind through the eye.
It comes to the heart, through the nose and the
    fingertips.

The old poet had it right.
"Do not go gentle..."
Even here in this moment of doubt
I don't give up.
I do not go gentle,
Down by two in the bottom of the 9th,
Two out,
Two on,
Two strikes.
I will take one more god damned pitch!

And even if I fail,
We will play again tomorrow.

The story of my life is told between parentheses
which you open and you close.
And inside those parentheses is one word.
It is (Hope).

*

Jack McCarthy

About 2 Poets
(by Thomas Lux)

Jack McCarthy is almost my exact contemporary and Jeffrey McDaniel is a generation younger. Despite this age difference, they share many things as poets: 1) neither fears being understood; 2) reading (or listening) to either, you believe a living, breathing human being is speaking to you; 3) each can be very serious, very funny; 4) neither writes incomprehensible poems so need not fear being written about incomprehensibly by an English professor; and 5) both are dead honest, and bear not a fiber of pretentiousness in their bodies.

McDaniel was my student as a freshman (1985). A few of the poems he wrote that year were good enough to make it into his very strong first book. He possesses one of the most extraordinary senses of metaphor in which I have ever taken delight. This ancient, fundamental poetic tool, metaphor is the only thing about poetry writing (Socrates said this a few thousand years ago) that can't be taught. Poetry, said Robert Frost, is one art form in which it is permitted to say one thing and mean another. Good metaphors do that and are at the same time instantaneously understood and never need a critic to explain to the poor dumb fuck reader (you or me!) what it means. McDaniel's work abounds in metaphor and simile, each or both always revealing an utterly lucid, rich, complex, passionate, contradictory, original way of confronting/praising this business of walking around on earth. Internationally known on the slam circuit and also highly regarded on the page, McDaniel has a foot firmly in both worlds. In fact, they're not two worlds, or shouldn't be. Let me state this as simply as I can: there are some bad slam poets, hundreds of decent slam poets, and a handful of brilliant ones. There are some bad "page" poets, hundreds of decent ones, and a handful of brilliant ones. For every self-indulgent and narcissistic slam or performance poet, there is a slim book of self-indulgent and narcissistic poems on a shelf somewhere. Bottom line: good poetry will stick around, bad/mediocre poetry will dry up and blow away. And that evaluation process begins with any writer's obituary. I've seen Jeffrey McDaniel's work grow richer with each book, grow wilder, grow more ambitious in his concerns (he looks outward at the world now, as well as inward), advancing in every way. He works like a demon. He loves poetry and not merely as the idea of being a poet. Read his books, listen to him read his poems aloud: it will change you. And do me a favor: stand in front of my grave in a few generations and say: "About McDaniel, pal, you were on the money."

Jack McCarthy, as I said, is a generation older than McDaniel. He is a vital part of a very large, needed, and necessary community of writers and poets in America who have no affiliation with colleges and universities. McCarthy has served his art form. The only ambition he seems to have is to tell the truth as best he can in poems. His work is direct, plainspoken, colloquial, authentic, lucid. Lucid, lucid again. Meaning: accessible (although I like Billy Collins's term for this kind of poetry—"hospitable"—just as much) enough, meaning complexity, textures, richness, reverberations, etc. Not meaning: too obvious, clichéd, easily paraphrased. Meaning: not being more afraid of being understood than afraid of being misunderstood. That kind of lucidity takes some guts. Have you ever considered how easy it is to be obscure? Have you ever wondered if obscurity is really often a cover-up for arbitrariness? You won't have this problem with McCarthy's work. You'll hear a natural, unforced voice in his poems, like listening to your best friend talk to you—urgently, calmly—while looking you straight in the eye. Of course, the poem will be much more articulate and rhythmical and less redundant than your best friend. That's what good writing does: it creates a kind of illusion. If you are watching a play, for example, and you are conscious every minute that you are watching someone act and that you are watching a play, then most likely the actor is doing a poor job and most likely the writer too. You get lost in reading or listening to Jack McCarthy's poems. Lost in characters, the story, the voice—so human, so alive. His poems are hard not to read. Only a real poet has as much forgiveness, as much generosity, as much crankiness as McCarthy. And forget the "at my grave" business. Read these poets now.

jack mcCarthy

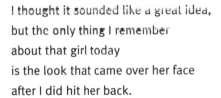

*hear...

track 32

Careful What You Ask For

I was just old enough
to be out on the sidewalk by myself,
and every day I would come home crying,
beaten up by the same little girl.

I was Jackie, the firstborn,
the apple of every eye,
gratuitous meanness bewildered me,
and as soon as she'd hit me,
I'd bawl like a baby.

I knew that boys were not supposed to cry,
but they weren't supposed to hit girls either,
and I was shocked when my father said,
"Hit her back."

I thought it sounded like a great idea,
but the only thing I remember
about that girl today
is the look that came over her face
after I did hit her back.

She didn't cry; instead
her eyes got narrow and I thought,
"Jackie, you just made a terrible mistake,"
and she really beat the crap out of me.
It was years before I trusted my father's advice
    again.

I eventually learned to fight—
enough to protect myself—
from girls—
but the real issue was the crying,
and that hasn't gone away.

Oh, I don't cry any more,
I don't sob, I don't make noise,
I just have hair trigger tearducts, and always
at all the wrong things: supermarket openings;
the mayor cutting the ribbon on the bridge.

In movies I despise the easy manipulation
that never even bothers to engage my feelings,
it just comes straight for my eyes,
but there's not a damn thing I can do about it,
and I hate myself for it.

The surreptitious nose blow a discreet
four minutes after the operative scene;
my daughters are on to me, my wife;
they all know exactly when to give me that quick,
sidelong glance. What must they think of me?

In real life I don't cry anymore
when things hurt. Never a tear at seventeen
when my mother died, my father.
I never cried for my first marriage.

But today I often cry when things turn out well:
an unexpected act of simple human decency;
new evidence, against all odds,
of how much someone loves me.

I think all this is why I never wanted a son.
I always supposed my son would be like me,
and that when he'd cry it would bring back
every indelible humiliation of my own life,

and in some word or gesture
I'd betray what I was feeling,
and he'd mistake, and think I was ashamed of
    him.
He'd carry that the rest of his life.

Daughters are easy: you pick them up,
you hug them, you say, "There there.
Everything is going to be all right."
And for that moment you really believe
that you can make enough of it right

enough. The unskilled labor of love.
And if you cry a little with them for all
the inevitable gratuitous meannesses of life,
that crying is not to be ashamed of.

But for years my great fear was the moment
I might have to deal with a crying son.
But I don't have one.
We came close once, between Megan and
    Kathleen;
the doctors warned us there was something
    wrong,

and when Joan went into labor they said
the baby would be born dead.
But he wasn't: very briefly,
before he died, I heard him cry.

*

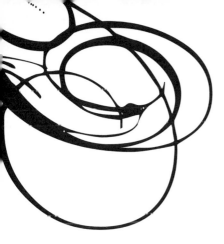

Cartalk: A Love Poem

The cars I drive
    don't look like much I will admit,
    but mostly they've got engines that won't
    quit
    this side of a nuclear explosion.

The Shitbox Mystique: when new friends
    point at dents, concerned, and ask,
    "What happened to your car?" I answer,
    "It was like that
    when I bought it."

When I met Carol she was driving
    a pretty good car,
    except for the air-conditioner,
    which used to make the engine overheat.
    Carol also brought into my life
    her son Seth and her mechanic, Peter—
    that's another feature
    of the Mystique, your mechanic
    becomes part of your family,
    we see more of Peter than we do of Seth,
    we invited him to our wedding—
    though I'll admit, Peter wasn't actually
    in the wedding, and Seth was.

Now Carol likes nice things,
    but what with college bills and all,
    a couple years with me
    and her blue Subaru
    went downhill fast
    and I got to see a new
    side of her, that her idea of a good day
    is breaking down outside a gas
    station.

Eventually the engine started
    overheating even without
    the air-conditioner; in fact
    the only way to keep the temperature
    out of the red zone on a hot day
    was to turn the heat on.
    I don't think Carol's mother
    ever really bought
    the unlikely physics of that;
    I think she thought we were
    trying to make her and Ed
    go home to California.

When you've got
    two people driving shitboxes
    you get to make some interesting decisions
    like which one to take to Connecticut.
    One has no windshield fluid
    because the plastic thing leaks
    and Peter hasn't been able to find
    a used one that fits;
    the other has something really scary
    going on with steering
    but we take it anyway,
    because on the map
    the road to Connecticut
    looks pretty straight.

Sometimes I get home from work
and Carol's ecstatic.
"Jack, I met the most wonderful
towtruck driver today. We towed
the car to Peter's,
and he brought me back
all the way to the door.
We had the most incredible conversation!
He's a very unusual person."

Right, Carol; like you're not.
A couple years with me she's on
a firstname basis with every
towtruck driver in Middlesex County.
Triple-A has us on speed-dial.

One time we were driving
somewhere together and she reflected,
"You know, if your first marriage
had worked out better, you
wouldn't have been available
for me. And vice versa."

I thought what a classic she is,
the miles look good on her;
but both of us came as is,
with dented fenders, and random
detritus in the trunk, and I said,
"It's as if we both broke down
outside the same gas station
at the same time."

And she smiled
and then she laughed,
and then we both laughed,
a long soft asynchronous laugh
like the ticking of an engine it will take
a nuclear blast
to stop.

*

degrees of Difficulty

(by Jack McCarthy)

The first time I attended the Boston Poetry Slam, it was still at the Bookcellar, it hadn't even moved to the Cantab Lounge yet. I brought a poem that night that I was really proud of. It was in rhyme and meter, and it was really clever, killer punchline. I still do it occasionally, and when I do it today, it works well.

But that night it didn't work. I lost the audience halfway through. When I got to my final punchline, only about four people were still with me. One of them was Patricia Smith, and she gave me a good shout out. But for most of the audience, I was a waste of time.

A young guy followed me. He did a long, rambling monologue about hitch-hiking across the country. It was funny in places, it was touching, it was good; and it could just as easily have been a short essay as a poem. The audience loved it. Hell, for that matter, *I* loved it. But I was hurt. I thought, "Why do they like what he did so much more than what I did? What I did was *so much more difficult*."

The answer that immediately flashed before my eyes, like those news bulletins that stream above Times Square, was, "So what? Audiences do not award any points for Degree of Difficulty." What we do is not a diving competition. It is a competition for the hearts and minds of a live audience, and the key to their hearts and minds is their attention. In order to hold their attention, we have to make some concessions.

Does this mean "dumbing down?" At its worst, yes. But I always answer that charge this way: what if you could write a poem that would get a 29.7 (let's say) at

Nationals, and then be published in *Best American Poetry* of the year? Would that be a kickass poem, or what? Would that not be a poem worth writing? If anybody answers that question "No," that person is beyond talking to. And I maintain that that's the poem we should always be hoping to write. Granted, not all material lends itself to that aspiration. But a Mack Dennis haiku is a step in the right direction.

Why does the poem I did that night at the Bookcellar work for me these days when it didn't work then? Because today, I have a reputation. Audiences trust that if they stay with me, I'll reward them. So they'll go a lot further with me before they tune me out. I think audiences today often tune out rhyme and meter. I think it's because there aren't many poets in our generation who handle rhyme and meter well. Billy Collins says he doesn't allow first-year poetry students to write in rhyme and meter because he feels they make it too easy to think you've written a poem, when you really haven't said anything worth saying. We see a lot of that with beginners.

But I've also seen audiences tune out people who handled rhyme and meter very well, and I suspect there's a very ungenerous reason for that. I sometimes feel myself thinking, "This guy probably thinks we should all write in rhyme and meter, that what I write really isn't poetry at all." And thinking that, I confess that I am hoping this guy fails with the audience. Yes, I know, it is unworthy, and when I see it happening I often go out of my way to tell the guy how much I admired what he accomplished in the poem. But I don't think I'm the only one in the audience who had that ungenerous feeling, and I suspect that it contributes to an anti-form bias among slammers and open-mikers. It's a bias that is usually justified; but I make an effort to keep my ears open for the exceptions, the rare contemporaries who handle the forms well.

In case it got lost in the shuffle, let me repeat that one sentence I promised you back at the beginning: Audiences do not award any points for Degree of Difficulty.

QUESTIONS FOR DE
WHAT TO CALL THEM?
PROP DEFINITION GO WITH OTHER DEFIN?
DISCUSSION OF PROPS AFTER RULE
ACCOMODATING BAN ON SACRIFICE
IS "RANK SCORE" CLEAR?
MOVE DEFINITIONS TO THE END

The Rules of the Na...

at least, the ones we agree...

I have to submit to much in order to pacify the touchy tribe of poets.

—Horace, 14 B.C.

WITHOUT THE HELP OF A W... FORCE.

FOREWORD

, PRESENTED AND APPROVED AT THE SLAMMASTER'S MEETING IN APRIL,

This collection of rules is not intended to put an end to the healthy controversy that been a part of the national slam community. If we took all the interpretation out of t on earth would we talk about? And yet, if the same rules were always worded the sa year to year, many arguments could be avoided. That's what this is: an attempt to a

omit?

The Passion Tree

This California Live Oak at the end
of my block looks like a couple
mid-fuck: ankles, thighs, groin, hips
entwined, forming a single trunk,
erupting into two separate bodies:
a damsel tilted back, the green breeze
of her hair, fingers gripping the triceps
of a lad thrusting, his rainbow spine
in a perpetual state of *timber*. Most trees
are only visible from the knees up,
calves unraveled in dirt, shoes fallen off.
Not this one. I keep a tiny piece
of its bark under my pillow. I stuff
its leaves in my underpants. I sleep
naked in its branches, hoping to wake
with its initials carved into my shoulder.

*

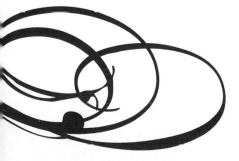

Dear America

I am but a riverboat—hopelessly in touch
with my inner canoe. On the first day of nursery
school, I cried in mother's arms. It wasn't
separation anxiety. I was scared she would
come back. In high school, I was voted *most
   likely
to secede*. In college, I took so many drugs
the professors looked at samples of my urine
just to know what books I'd been reading.
I'm a narcissist trapped in the third person.
The sound of my own head being shaved
is my all-time favorite song. I stop people
on the street, show them pictures of myself
as a child, ask *have you seen this boy?
He's been missing for a long time*. His eyes
are the last swig of whiskey before stumbling
out of a bar on a sunny afternoon. His cheeks
are twirling ballerinas. His cheeks are revolving
doors. I'm all out of cheeks to turn. I'm all
out of cheeks. My ego is a spiral staircase
inside a tornado. My eyebrows are that furry
feeling you get in your gut when you're about
to tell a lie. My tongue is a dolphin

passed out in an elevator. My tongue is a red
    carpet
I only roll out for you. My penis is a wise ass
in the back of a classroom who doesn't know
the answer, but sticks his hand up anyway.
My heart hangs in my chest like a Salem witch.
My heart is a turtle ripped from its shell.
My heart is a street so dark nymphomaniacs
are afraid to kiss. My heart, America, my heart.

The Abandoned
Factory of Sense

When I was a kid, my mother
had the prettiest face: a smile
that could pry open the hearts
of construction workers, eyes
bright as a Kennedy's future,
lips red as a robin feather floating
in a bathtub filled with milk,
and everybody loved her.
But when we came home,
she'd take off her face and hang it
on a special pole by her bed,
and if I got scared, or sad, or just
wanted the lollipop of her attention,
she couldn't give it, because
she didn't have any eyes, or
mouth to teach the word *stop*.
No lips to kiss me goodnight,
or nose to smell the roses
bunched up in my fist.

*

The Foxhole Manifesto

"There are no atheists in foxholes."

—old Christian proverb

The first god I remember was a Santa Claus god,
   who you only
turned to around Christmas time,
who you tried to butter up, and then got mad at if
   you didn't
get what you wanted.
That didn't make sense. I knew if there was a
   god, he could see
through us, like we were made
out of cellophane, like he could stare directly into
   our hearts,
the way we look into an aquarium,
like he'd know what was floating around in there,
   like he might be
the one feeding it.
Then there were those people who used god to
   threaten you,
saying *you better*
be careful—god's watching, like god was a
   badass hillbilly

sitting in some cloud
with a pair of binoculars, a cotton candy beard, a
   six pack,
and a shot-gun.
Then I saw people who had Jesus' name on their
   bumper sticker,
like he was running for president.
And sometimes those people with Jesus on their
   bumper sticker
would cut you off
on the freeway and give you the finger, which is
   very different
from lending you a hand.
Then there were people on television, dressed in
   weird clothes
and scary make-up, swearing
they had the secret to god, like god was a
   keyhole and their eyeball
was pressed to it, and if I just
gave 'em some money they'd let me look, and
   then I could see god
just hanging around in his boxer shorts,
and though I liked the idea of spying on god, I
   began to wonder
if the world would be a healthier place
if the Romans had just put up with Jesus and let
   him die of old age.
And then there were the football players,
   kneeling down in front
of everybody, thanking god,
like he was their best friend, but then they'd
   jump up and spike
the ball, yell *I'm number one,*
and I'd be confused, because if you're number
   one, then

what number is god?
Then I saw politicians trotting god out on a leash,
    like a racehorse
they wanted to hop on
and ride to the finish line. But if they lost it would
    be god's fault,
and god would be the donkey
they'd pin all their problems on, and that was
    very nice of god:
to be both a race horse and a donkey.
And then there were those who said *you better
    be good on Earth
if you wanna get into heaven*,
like heaven was the United States, and Earth was
    Mexico, and angels
were border patrol. Like when you die
you sit in a parked car on the outskirts of
    heaven, the engine idling,
your soul in the back seat in one of those
    kennels
used to carry small dogs on airplanes, as you
    listen on the radio to all
the people you ever wronged testify against you.
And then there was the church, which was like
    this cafeteria, where
they served god to you on these very
ungodlike plates, but I wanted my god pure, and
    not watered down
by human beings, so I just had one of those
catastrophe gods—you know, the one you only
    turn to in an emergency,
like god's the national guard you call in
to clean up the earthquake of your life. So I got
    drunk one night,
drove home, passed out behind the wheel,

woke, going sixty straight at a brick wall,
    slammed the brakes, heart
banging like a wrecking ball in my chest,
staring at death's face in the bricks, close enough
    to see we had
the same cheekbones.
Now I have a god who's like a mechanic who can
    fix anything,
so when I wanna chew somebody's head off
like a saltwater taffy, or amputate my DNA, or
    open my wrists
like windows that have been painted shut,
I just put my soul into a box, like a busted com-
    puter, and haul it in.
And he never asks to see my paperwork,
or says my warranty has expired. And I walk out
    feeling better.
And I don't care if he doesn't exist.

*

Around & IN the Scene

(by Bob Holman)

The Nuyorican Poets Café, where I'd first heard rap, was closed in the '80s because of AIDS, crack, and gentrification. I started to think about opening my own club. This led to my investigation of what had happened to the Nuyorican, and eventually leading the effort that reopened the Café. The vectors were lined up and ready for the explosion that was the Café in those early years of the '90s. Multi-culti was energizing. The Nuyorican was an open platform for these voices. Hip hop was poetry here; performance was poetry too. The Nuyorican aesthetic was open, street, loud. It was the perfect patria dish for slam.

We'd been talking about how to fill up the programming at the Café when I spied an intriguing article about poetry slams in Chicago—populist, rowdy, with a TV game show format, in a word, "wow!" I found myself in the Green Mill a few weeks later and was mesmerized by Marc Smith's show. I saw the poetry slam as a perfect form to attract an audience, to give poets, especially new poets, a chance to read their words in front of an audience of strangers, and to have all this happen in an entertaining, challenging, and controversial fashion. As we divvied up the Café week, I picked Fridays at ten for the slam, which is when they are still held today.

That first cold winter at the Café, Steve Cannon, still sighted, brought heckling to an art form. The word got out that the Nuyorican was a safe place full of risk, a place where you could get cheap beer and refuel your imagination, where you could have a good time without turning your mind off, where you could go to a poetry reading without having to admit that you were going to a poetry reading—you were going to a slam!

"Every slam a finality." —Bob Kaufman. Every slam an event, a trial, a roller derby, a poetry mixer, a crossover dream. Here was a chance to go out for a night and hear poets of every description, every stage of development, and have judges, whose only qualification be that they are unqualified, give numerical ratings to the poetry. And the crowds grew and grew. For seven years at the Poetry Project, I had written weekly press releases that had been like sending paper airplanes into an abyss. Great readings, great poets, no press. But now, with a scene whose undercurrent was social change, with a poetry reading where you could describe the slam instead of printing/analyzing the poetry, you had a ready-made success. The Café took off. The press came to the slams on their own. But while it might have been the form that caused the hoopla, it was the content—the art, the talent and skills—of the poets that gave a backbone of integrity to the carnival of slam. Paul Beatty was the first Grand Slam Champ at the Café. I'd just won a New York Foundation for the Arts grant, so I plunked that down for Paul's prize—a book of his poems. The idea was for the slam to feed back into other poetic traditions—text, *par ejemplo!* In our tiny town, once the connection between spoken word/hip hop/performance/slam/political verse had begun, it completely swept away other poetic forces. And why not? In a world where the Yale Younger Poets Prize meant you were under forty and often went to a thirty-nine-year-old on a tenure track, all of a sudden the Café's younger poets were seventeen-year-old high school students.

There was a hunger to hear the single voice of the poet, speaking from the heart. From the slams and hip hop and performance, The Nuyorican Poets Café Live touring company was born, spreading words across the country and around the globe.

Slam remains the most energetic grassroots arts movement in the country. I'm especially impressed at the way that Youth Speaks and the Writers Corps have been able to use slam to engage high schoolers in the arts, in self-statement, in a way to bite onto culture with your own culture. The World Heavyweight Bout in Taos has met slam head-on and proved that there's more than one way to win a poetry contest—and generate a poetry audience.

And I continue to devote myself to the job. I teach at Bard College, I work with City Lore and Poets House to find the international connections at the biennial The Peoples Poetry Gathering, and I'm hard at work at the Bowery Poetry Club, where poetry is the main event every day. Come for the coffee, stay for the poetry. With Luis and Trini Rodriguez's Tia Chucha Cafe Cultural in Sylmar, California, I see a movement of poets grabbing their own space, creating places for poetry that live in the world while maintaining a poetic economy.

The divisions are cracking now that poets are finding a toehold in the culture. We can spread out a bit, enjoy each other, share respect, listen. That's my job now: to bring the orbits together, let the poets be heard, the first time since Plato exiled us from the Republic. Ah, but poetry lives on! These many forms prove its vitality. Recently on the Poets House Bridge Walk, Marie Howe, Ed Hirsch, Willie Perdomo, and Galway Kinnell read. It was great! The bridge was not the only metaphor in town, but it was more than a mile long. Kenneth Koch read at the Bowery Poetry Club, a Poetry Society of America event, which seemed to bring a circle together for me. I turned on the Walt Whitman Lite-Brite on the side of the stage and said, "Oh Walt! I love you!"

Bob Holman,
Taylor Mali, and
Gary Mex Glazner

bob holman

track 26

DisClaimer

We begin each SLAM! with a Disclaimer:

As Dr. Willie used to say,
We are gathered here today
because we are not gathered
somewhere else today, and
we don't know what we're doing
so you do—the Purpose of SLAM!
being to fill your hungry ears
with Nutritious Sound/Meaning Constructs,
Space Shots into Consciousness
known hereafter as Poems, and
not to provide a Last Toehold
for Dying Free Enterprise Fuck 'em
for a Buck'em Capitalism'em. We disdain
competition and its ally war
and are fighting for our lives
and the spinning

of poetry's cocoon of action
in your dailiness. We refuse
to meld the contradictions but
will always walk the razor
for your love. "The best poet
always loses" is no truism of SLAM!
but is something for you
to take home with you like an image
of a giant condor leering over
a salty rock. Yes, we must destroy
ourselves in the constant
reformation that is this very moment,
and propel you to write the poems
as the poets read them, urge you
to rate the judges as they trudge
to their solitary and lonely numbers,
and bid you dance or die between sets.

*

Praise Poem for Slam: Why Slam Causes Pain and Is a Good Thing

"—sigh. why does this have to be such a pain?"
—Charles Ellik

Because Slam is Unfair.

Because Slam is too much fun.

Because poetry.

Because rules.

Because poetry rules.

Because the poetry gets lost.

Because poetry is an endangered species Slam finds and revivifies.

Because you cannot reduce a poem to its numerological equivalent.

Because hey it's poetry in everyday life every Sunday at 7:30 PM.

Because I can do that.

Because everybody's voice is heard.

Because Old White Guys as usual.

Because it's the opposite that includes the opposite.

Because do not institutionalize the anti-institution!

Because it's meant for middle and high schoolers so they get their adrenaline poetry shots.

Because Pepsi and Nike have conflicting ideas about the team uniforms.

Because competitive.

Because Allen Ginsberg says, "Slam! Into the Mouth of the Dharma!"

Because Gregory Corso says, "Why do you want to hang out with us old guys? If I was young, I'd be going to the Slam!"

Because Bob Kaufman writes, "Each Slam/a finality."

Because Patricia Smith has more truth in her little finger than entire *Boston Globe* front page.

Because Marc Smith and because Chicago.

Because Nuyorican Poets Cafe and multi-culti.

Because Taos World Heavyweight Championship Poetry Bout.

Because rap is poetry, and hip hop is culture.

Because three minute pop song.

Because the point is not the points.

Because audience.

Because heckling.

Because judges selected whimsically are instant experts.

Because Dewey Decimal System of Slam Scorification reduces possibility of Ties and Dreaded Sudden-Death Spontaneous Haiku Overtime Round.

Because the National Slam is summer boot camp for poets.

Because first six years only women win Indy Slam Champ Boot.

Because local heroes finally have national community.

Because democratization of art.

Because Best Poet Always Loses.

Because cool mediaization of poetry is rooted in hot live performance of poetry.

Because when in the course it looks like poetry is disappearing, the furious uproar of the Word will not be stilled.

Because William Carlos Williams wrote, "It's hard to find the news in poetry," but we say, we've got news for you.

Because performance is a see-through page, and the oral tradition a hidden book

Because it's called Slam.

Performance Poem

"Voices. Voices. Listen, my heart, as only
saints have listened; until the gigantic call lifted
    them
off the ground; yet they kept on, impossibly,
kneeling and didn't notice at all:
so complete was their listening."

—Rilke

He's diving off the front of the stage!
You better bring the house lights up some,
The audience can't see him.
He's still screaming,
Screaming and dancing
And he's twirling the mike—
I dunno, should we turn off the mike?
I dunno, turn it up?
He's running around, he's twirling and
He's still like reading.
The book is in his hands, sort of, the people
Seem to like it, they're into it—
Maybe it's part of the act.

If it's part of the act he shoulda told us!
Now he's in the back of the house—he's
Still going strong. This is pretty
Amazing. I've never seen anything
Like this! He's running out
Of the theater—I can still hear him screaming
In the lobby. He's back in the house!
(What's he saying?—It's something about
It sounds like "lake snore freedom"....
I dunno. "Breaking down reason"?)
Oh shit! Oh shit oh shit—he's got a gun!

Christ! wait—awww, it's just one of those pop
     guns.
Shoots like firecrackers or popcorn or—
What about the hat? Still wearing the hat.
Holy—he's dying now, I mean he's acting like
     that,
Like he's dying. This is it for poetry in this house
     man,
I've had it.

He's just lying there.
The audience is wailing, they're keening
You know, like at a wake. No, I do not think
He's really dead. He's getting back up, see, I told
You—it's all part of the act!

It's all part of the end of the world.
What am I, the guy's father?
Come here! Look at the monitor yourself
He's ditched the mike somewhere,
Should I go get the mike?
Look! oh my God—he's, what's it called,
He's going up, he's levitating!
Holy shit! The roof, the roof is going up
Music is coming in
The crowd's up outta the chairs, man this is it
This is it I'm telling you—
Raising the fucking roof is what he's doing!
Now he's back on the stage with his poetry stuff
Yeah heh heh yeah,

He never left the stage
It's what his poem was about
I'm just saying what he's saying
Through the headset
Yeah, he's good
He's pretty good all right
But I could write something like that
Anybody could write something like that

Peter Meets the Wolf

The way a tree falls
when lightning strikes it,
is what he was
to him. And he to him,
a flute. The way reeds
blow in a howl.
It was like that
for many months. Him
falling down
and the other
making music
from the timber.

*

Hansel Tells Gretel
of the Witch

How easy she was to please with the stories
I told through the slats of her cage.

When we stuffed our pockets with berries
And walked like ducks to fallen father's cheeks.

Or the time I thought the birds despised us
when they nibbled our bread

and left stones in our footprints.
Then nightfall and no creek to follow—

all stars extinguished in the too tall branches
and whispers of stalking owls.

Stumbling when the bats fluttered sideways
round our ears till we saw

the flicker from her half-opaque windows.
Do you recall feasting off her flower pots

of chocolate and freshly baked pretzel stems,
falling asleep in a spell of rice pudding?

What I remember is waking to a sweat and
    licorice
scent. Of course I knew we'd die.

The twisted hair barrette and tattered sock,
soiled beneath my head,

were just reminders of what would come.
As she struck the match, I asked

that she not kill me or you. And in her eyes,
I saw those unforgiven ghosts.

Children like us, playing freeze tag in
    darkness,
charred and vanished.

From her final breath, I heard those
muffled screams, a sudden gust-like tug,

parentless and bewildered
their pitch deafened by the kiln's hot hand.

*

taylor mali

*hear...

track 29

How to Write a Political Poem

for my soon-to-be-former friends at Bar 13

However it begins, it's gotta be loud
And then it's gotta get a little bit louder.
Because this is how you write a political poem
and how you deliver it with power.

Mix current events with platitudes of
    empowerment.
Wrap it up in rhyme or rhyme it up in rap until it
    sounds true.

Glare until it sinks in.

Because somewhere in Florida, votes are still
    being counted.
I said somewhere in Florida, votes are still being
    counted!

See, that's the Hook, and you gotta' have a Hook.
More than the look, it's the hook that is the most
    important part.
The hook has to hit and the hook's gotta fit.
Hook's gotta hit hard in the heart.

Because somewhere in Florida, votes are still
    being counted.

TOP SECRET

slam strategies

And Dick Cheney is peeing all over himself in
    spasmodic delight.
Make fun of politicians, it's easy, especially with
    Republicans
like Rudy Giuliani, Colin Powell, and...Al Gore.
Create fatuous juxtapositions of personalities
    and political philosophies
as if communism were the opposite of
    democracy,
as if we needed Darth Vader, not Ralph Nader.

Peep this: When I say "Call,"
you all say, "Response."

Call! *Response!* Call! *Response!* Call!

Amazing Grace, how sweet the—

Stop in the middle of a song that everyone knows
    and loves.
This will give your poem a sense of urgency.
Because there is always a sense of urgency in a
    political poem.

There is no time to waste!
Corruption doesn't have a curfew,
greed doesn't care what color you are
and the New York City Police Department
is filled with people who wear guns on their hips
and carry metal badges pinned over their hearts.
Injustice isn't injustice it's just in us as we are
    just in ice.
That's the only alienation of this alien nation
in which you either fight for freedom
or else you are free and dumb!

And even as I say this somewhere in Florida,
    votes are
still being counted.

And it makes me wanna beat box!

Because I have seen the disintegration of
    gentrification
and can speak with great articulation
about cosmic constellations, and atomic
    radiation.
I've seen D. W. Griffith's *Birth of a Nation*
but preferred *101 Dalmatians.*
Like a cross examination, I will give you the
    explanation

of why *SlamNation* is the ultimate manifestation
of poetic masturbation and egotistical
    ejaculation.

And maybe they are still counting votes
    somewhere in Florida,
but by the time you get to the end of the poem it
    won't matter anymore.

Because all you have to do is close your eyes,
lower your voice, and end by saying:

the same line three times,
the same line three times,
the same line three times.

 *

BY TAYLOR
MALI

Like Lilly Like Wilson

I'm writing the poem that will change the world,
   and it's Lilly Wilson at my office door.
Lilly Wilson, the recovering like addict, the worst
   I've ever seen.
So, like, bad the whole eighth grade started
   calling her Like Lilly Like Wilson Like.
Until I declared my classroom a Like-Free Zone,
   and she could not speak for days.

But when she finally did, it was to say,
Mr. Mali, this is...so hard.
Now I have to think before I...say anything.

Imagine that, Lilly.

It's for your own good.
Even if you don't like...it.

I'm writing the poem that will change the world,
   and it's Lilly Wilson at my office door.
Lilly is writing a research paper for me about how
   homosexuals shouldn't be allowed to adopt
   children.
I'm writing the poem that will change the world,
   and it's Like Lilly Like Wilson at my office
   door.

She's having trouble finding sources, which is to
   say, ones that back her up.
They all argue in favor of what I thought I was
   against.

And it took four years of college, three years of
   graduate school, and every incidental
   teaching experience I have ever had to let out
   only,

Well, that's a real interesting problem, Lilly. But
   what do you propose to do about it? That's
   what I want to know.

And the eighth-grade mind is a beautiful thing;
Like a new-born baby's face, you can often see it
   change before your very eyes.

I can't believe I'm saying this, Mr. Mali, but I think
   I'd like to switch sides.

Beau Sia, Taylor Mali, Bob Holman, Regie Cabico, and Evert Eden

And I want to tell her to do more than just believe
   it, but to enjoy it!
That changing your mind is one of the best ways
   of finding out whether or not you still have
   one.
Or even that minds are like parachutes, that it
   doesn't matter what you pack them with so
   long as they open at the right time.
O God, Lilly, I want to say you make me feel like a
   teacher, and who could ask to feel more than
   that?
I want to say all this but manage only, Lilly, I am
   like so impressed with you!

So I finally taught somebody something, namely,
   how to change her mind.
And learned in the process that if I ever change
   the world it's going to be one eighth grader at
   a time.

Howl

howl

allen ginsberg
told me
that I was beautiful
in a new york city cafe
and I thought
he was trying to
pick me up.

you can imagine how arrogant chinese boys in
new york get about love when old, gay white men
are involved.

exactly eleven months later,
he died.

the time between point A and B
can be measured in days,
but friendship hates math,
and so the sum of experiences
between two people
is not a sum,
it's eating blintzes under trees
learning how cezanne chose to color,
and it's
sitting in bed,
debating the value of failure in one's life,
and it's seeing allen
read one last time
in front of 680 nyu kids that
had no idea
he would spend the next two weeks in boston,
starting negotiations with death.

my friend is dead
and I don't know how
to approach the subject.

Beau Sia

my generation has no starving, hysterical
nakeds.
I'm a member of the fame whore, superstar-at-
any-cost-we-could-give-a-fuck-about-a-fuck-
because-teen-angst-isn't-enough-anymore-
our-self-absorbed-natures-have-overkilled-
into-egomaniacal-dynamo-rage generation,
and we don't know
the first thing
about the words,
"selfless," and "give."

I mean,
fuck the fact that he's gay,
a beatnik,
and that even I get bored
with his poetry,
the ginz made tibet a cause to believe in,
pushed the angry buttons of politicians for
four decades,
and set fire to one hundred and eighteen
million minds in this world,
becoming lou reed, bob dylan,
billy burroughs, and my answer
to the question,
"who has influenced you in this life?"

sure, some days
he was an asshole,
but most of us aren't in the public eye enough
to be caught during our asshole moments.
but for each of those asshole moments,
there is the simple beauty
of him cooking mushroom omelettes,
and him exposing me to the ways
of buddhism (that which my ancestors
taught him),
and his wily, old man eyes
correcting me and saying,
"you have a long way to go if you want to be a
good writer."

don't try and dull my memories of him.

at point A
I ran with his mind in a 13th st. loft
because his legs
were no longer capable
of adventures on foot,
to point B,
when I sat silent by the phone,
listening to him say
four days before his death
that he thought
he had another month.

point B to point C is a distance I'm not sure I'll
ever reach,
as I try to find straight lines,
reading his work in barnes & noble,
and
remembering how he'd tell me
about his first connections to kerouac
with reverence,
and
I don't know if I'll ever understand
the scope of the words, "death,"
or "good-bye,"
but I'm getting that little ache under the ribcage
from loss
and the need to finally
tell a friend,
"I love you."

Love

I think love
is the most beautiful thing
in the world
and I don't give a fuck,
because I have no original ideas.
I'm a pathetic man
whose goal is to read poetry
to get women
to fall in love with him,
and you'd think I was reprimanding myself
and revealing my horrible dark side
by saying that,
but I was really saying,

"women who hear this, fall in love with me,
or else."

because that's what it comes down to—
an ultimatum,
life or death,
and sure,
maybe I'm being extreme,
but you tell me that things aren't extreme.
jesus,
I've seen a man Jack-off to a gap window display,
so don't tell me
that love isn't important.
and maybe you don't get me yet,
that's okay,
you don't have to understand all of it,
just listen to the crucial 12 percent of my words,
like,
"fuck," and "ass," and
"ride my dongstick you naughty schoolgirl!"
because in a poem about love
we all need to know
the relevant things,
because we are all looking
for the complete definition
of love,
if only we could open up
our encyclopedia brittanicas
and know,
but love isn't that easy.

they say cupid loved *freaks and geeks*,
and when the show was cancelled
cupid cried and cried and cried
and decided that he was gonna fuck up
all of humanity,
and this is why china has trouble
with its birthrate,
and arkansas rhymes with date rape,
and the fat lypo-sucked out of california
could be its own island,
but this isn't a poem about geography.

this is a poem about love,
the bane of my existence,
the reason why I hate valentine's day
and halloween,
which is about ghosts,
and I think you know where I'm going here.

I'm going to the land of
girlfriends of halloween's pasts,
and maybe I've only got three girls
in this land,
but that doesn't mean that they don't bring their
friends,
who are the ghosts of girls
who have rejected me,
because girls rarely travel alone
in this land,

lydia is from this land.
I used to kiss her
while listening to the cure's
"just like heaven."
now I don't see her anymore,
so that song makes me sad.
why must we associate music
with our love lives?
I'm not trying to be profound here,
I'm just saying that
music takes me back,
way back,
and I can't explain the memory process involved
in that,
because I wasn't a psychology major,
and maybe my problem
with picking up women
has to do with me always asking them,
"yo, shorty! what's your major?"

but that only makes me as cheesy as 90 percent
of guys looking for women
and 72 percent of them have women,
so what's the deal here?

Maybe I shouldn't think of women
in terms of picking them up,
and maybe I should open up my sensitive side.
but really,
the sensitive side sucks!
I've been there!
you can only imagine
the kinds of sweaters they make you wear!

it's not fair.
love is not fair,
and war is not fair,
and I don't care what you say
about any of that,
I feel unloved.
I'm sorry I need people to tell me I'm cool.
I'm just that way.
aren't you?
am I the only one?
I know that I can't be that misunderstood,
but you don't want to understand me.

you just want to hear the part
about my small dick again,
because the asian man
will always be plagued by
this rumor,
until he is brave enough to whip it out on stage
and say,
"ha! we are gigantic!"

honestly,
this is not
the direction
I wanted to take this poem.
I just want to be in the arms of my true love,
in a house, in a room, in a wonderful,
perfect world,
with our two children, a boy and a girl,
helga and lamar.

but maybe I shouldn't have said this.
woody allen taught us that marriage
is the death trap.
I'm almost as old as his girlfriend.
she could be the long lost sister
I've been looking for.
maybe my mother gave her away
when we lived in china—
wait!
I never lived in china.
I've begun lying in this poem,
when all I wanted to do
was talk about love
for 3.2 minutes
and then come to a conclusion
defining love
within this poem,
but I don't have any answers,
and I'm looking for help from anyone,
because love
has got me fucked up and dying,
because I feel retardo
without anyone to hold me,
and maybe that's sentimental,
but what's wrong with sentimental?

all I'm saying is
"someone. love me."

*

And Then She

A man will sell you your death from the trunk of a compact car
hugging the curb of an ordinary boulevard, he'll hand you the gun
and his fingers are like teeth, then seeing the dead end
in your eyes he asks "You ain't gon' do nothing stupid, is
you sister?" and you suspect he may be the second coming
because he does not wait for an answer. The gun is tiny enough
to be a toy, black to the point of blue, an oil stink to the battered
metal. But once it's really mine, I swagger toward my own
destruction, legs lazy and bowed as a cowboy's. I practice seducing
the slick barrel, close my lips around the gun's hot eye and breathe in,
lacking the dim commitment to drag the trigger backwards,
hoping to simply persuade the bullet through the chamber and send it
searing through my landscape to my toes, convinced that a complete death
is the only cleansing the world will accept. Or perhaps this ceasing
of self will just be a well-timed but gruesome hallelujah,
a tsk-tsk don't ya wish, a touché got her out the way,
a bloody period at the end of a fragment of a sentence:
And then she—
Journalists around the world celebrated as—
Contacted at her home in Chicago, her mother—
Or maybe my body, old friend that it is, will refuse to let loose my soul.
I will spend eternity pumping bullets into my head and the wind will
whistle through all those neat, perfect holes the way it whistles

over the bowed heads of flowers in a field.
I will keep living to see myself keep dying.
The boom and the backflip. The boom and the backflip.
My obituary humming in the bowels of newsroom computers,
expiration date changing with each fucked up kapow, each perfect hole.
Frustrated headline writers abandon all attempts at objectivity, write:
Disgraced Ousted Sinful Ex-columnist Just Doesn't Get It.

Accepting of the idea if not the execution, I hide the gun
on a shelf behind one painfully alphabetized row of poetry volumes:
The One Day by Donald Hall, *Old and New Poems* by Donald Hall,
The Museum of Clear Ideas by Donald Hall, and *To Put the Mouth To*,
an exquisite and quite hurtful book by someone named Judith Hall,
which contains a poem which contains these lines:

Did I remind you how useful it is to declare
Your writing true? Let your voice break:
The horror, horror, harrowing:
How language cannot contain the wounds...
Your words in the mouths of stars who die,
Bleeding in oval shapes. The actors
Rarely die to make finales realistic.
You should ask if I enacted pain to—write,
Calling myself the victim-witness-priestess
Who knows she dies—is dying
Imperceptibly, her hand warmed by remote
Controls, switching channels. She controls
The news.

The gun bides its time while the phone keeps clanging,
it waits while television newsmen with an overflow of
canine teeth rap on my front door, it lives behind the rhymes
while poets choke the phone line with tears, while salt of the earth
is seduced, it lives there while I celebrate my 43rd birthday,
the occasion itself a glaring mistake. The gun learns to breathe

in the darkness, secure in its Donald Hall-way as guests suck sauce
from their fingers, armchair quarterbacks comment on how well I
seem to be holding up and backstabbers sharpen their vowels and
mentally price-tag my possessions—including the warm-blooded one—
and shake their asses to the strains of my impressive record collection.
The gun smells oilier, primes itself, woos me with a funk-filled
siren song: *Baby, bring your baaad ass on up heah.*
It knows I will climb the stairs to my office, take it from
its place on the shelf and lie on my back with dead summer air
drooping outside the shutters, *say goodnight gracie, good night gracie,*
and the unquestioning O of the barrel's end feeds me oxygen,
spits in necessary breath, and oh, in my head I write my ass off,
I invent a me who never existed, I fill her mouth with kickass quotes
instead of bullets, I'm *where oh I'm there with tears in my hair,*
proud owner of a gun that memorizes lines of poetry
and gets the last laugh by giving life instead of taking life away.
"You ain't gon' do nothing stupid, is you, sister?"
Yes. I am staying here, upright, unbroken, deserving of this air.

*

Building Nicole's Mama

For the 6th grade class of Lillie C. Evans School,
Liberty City, Miami

I am astounded at their mouthful names—
Lakinishia, Fumilayo, Chevellanie, Delayo—
their ragged rebellions and lip-glossed pouts,
and all those pants drooped as drapery.
I rejoice when they kiss my face, whisper wet
and urgent in my ear, make me their obsession
because I have brought them poetry.
They shout me raw, bruise my wrists with
pulling
and brashly claim me as mama as they
cradle my head in their little laps,
waiting for new words to grow in my mouth.
You. You. *You.*
Angry, jubilant, weeping writers—we are all
saviors, reluctant Hosannas in the limelight,
but you knew that, didn't you? Then let us
bless this sixth grade class, 40 nappy heads,
40 crackling voices, and all of them
raise their hands when I ask. They have all seen
the Reaper, grim in his heavy robe,

pushing the button for the dead project elevator,
begging for a break at the corner pawn shop,
cackling wildly in the back pew of the Baptist
   church.
I ask the death question and forty fists
punch the air, *me!, me!,* and O'Neal,
matchstick crack child, watched his mothers'
body become a claw and 9-year-old Tiko
   Jefferson,
barely big enough to lift the gun, fired a bullet
into his own throat after mama bended his back
with a lead pipe. Tamika cried into a sofa pillow
when daddy blasted mama into the north wall
of their cluttered one-room apartment,
Donya's cousin gone in a driveby. Dark window,
click, click, gone, says Donya, her tiny finger
a barrel, the thumb a hammer. I am astonished
at their losses—and yet when I read a poem
   about my own hard-eyed teenager, Jeffery
   asks
He is dead yet?
It cannot be comprehended,
my 18-year-old still pushing and pulling
his own breath. And those 40 faces pity me,
knowing that I will soon be as they are,
numb to our bloodied histories,
favoring the Reaper with a thumbs-up and a
   wink,
hearing the question and shouting *me, me,*
Miss Smith, I know somebody dead!
Can poetry hurt us? they ask me before
snuggling inside my words to sleep. *I love you,*
Nicole says, Nicole wearing my face,
pimples peppering her nose, and she is as black
as angels are. Nicole's braids clipped, their ends

kissed with match flame to seal them, and
can you teach me to write a poem about my
	mother?
I mean, you write about your daddy and he dead,
can you teach me to remember my mama?
A teacher tells me this is the first time Nicole
has admitted that her mother is gone,
murdered by slim silver needles and a stranger
rifling through her blood, the virus pushing
her skeleton through for Nicole to see.
And now this child with rusty knees and
mismatched shoes sees poetry as her scream
and asks me for the words to build her mother
again. Replacing the voice. Stitching on the lost
	flesh.
So poets,
as we pick up our pens,
as we flirt and sin and rejoice behind
	microphones—
remember Nicole.
She knows that we are here now,
and she is an empty vessel waiting to be filled.

And she is waiting.
And she
is waiting.
And she waits.

*

Patricia Smith

My Mother Learns English

An anxious immigrant at 64, my mother is learning English.
Pulling Sears Best cinnamon stockings to a roll beneath her knees,
sitting that Baptist ski slope of a hat on her head,
she rides the rattling El train to a steel spire in downtown Chicago,
pulls back her gulp as the glass elevator hurtles upward
and comes to sit at a gleaming oak table
across from a pinstriped benevolent white angel
who has dedicated two hours a week
to straightening the black, twisted tongues of the afflicted.
It is this woman's job to scrape the moist infection
of Aliceville, Alabama from my mother's throat.
"I want to talk right before I die," my mother says,
"Want to stop saying 'ain't' and 'I done been' like I don't have no sense.
I done lived too long to be stupid, acting like I just got off the boat."
My mother has never been on a boat.
But 50 years ago, a million of her, clutching strapped cloth suitcases
and peppery fried chicken in waxed bags,
stepped off the buses at the Greyhound depot in Chicago,
eagerly brushing the stubborn red dust from their shoes.
"We North now," they all said, still in their southern tongues,
as if those three words were vessels big enough to hold
it all, all those dreams with bulging seams, dreams
that spilled over the borders of sleeping, dreams that

hurt the eyes with their feverish glow, dreams that
got drunk on sweet water and whispered promises.
My mother's northern dreams were simple, but huge—
she thought it a modern miracle to live in a box
stacked upon other boxes, a tenement apartment where
every surface smelled of Lysol and effort, and plump
roaches, cross-eyed with spray, dragged themselves across
freshly washed dishes, dropped dizzily from the ceiling
into our food, our beds. Mama's huge dream required
starch stiff pinafores, orlon sweaters with stitched roses
and A-line skirts in the color of winter. There had to be

a tavern on the corner with a jukebox where men begged
forgiveness in gravel voices and a comfortable stool by
the door, where mama could sit and look like a Christian
who was just leaving. She needed a job that didn't involve
soil or branches, in a factory where she could work in a
straight line with other women, *repedida, repedida, repedida,*
no talking allowed, their heads drooping with dreams.
Within walking distance of wherever she lived, there had
to be a Baptist Church where she could pull on the white
gloves of service and wail to the rafters when she felt the
hot hand of the Holy Ghost pressing insistent at the small
of her back. Yes, Jesus had to be there—He had blessed
her journey so far, quickened her step, stroked her free
of the Delta. She was His child, building herself anew
here where the burning of her hair was a ritual and she'd
given up wearing pants because the Lord said she should.
Her dreams for the most part realized, my mother now busies
herself preparing for burial, stashing away a dollar here,
a dollar there, to pay for her own coffin, not wanting to bother
me, as she says, *with that nonsense.* She instructs me not to
spend lots of money putting her under, and once again sternly
relates the story of the dutiful daughter who neglected details,
so her dead mother's body was sent to church #1 while

everyone waited to mourn in church #2. *If that happened,*
chile, I'd be so embarrassed. No mother, I think, you would
be so dead, but I don't dare actually bring this to voice
because Annie Pearl Smith is not a fan of humor.
She is retired now after 40 years working in a candy factory,
making malted milk balls, hot dog gum and candy corn.
She'd been gone from the place for a year before she could
scrub the stark sugar smell out of her skin. When my father
was murdered, almost 25 years ago, mama and I gazed at
each other across a huge yawning chasm, we had no idea
one about the other. I had spent so many hopeful years
dousing my father in my dreams and he had listened

while my mother cursed a comb through my nappy hair,
nagged me to sit up straight, checked my grades, led me
to church, and grabbed the switch when I sassed.
She didn't talk unless talking was necessary.
Now she says it hurt her that I gave him everything.
So, of course, now I want to get to know her.
I know she doesn't believe men ever landed on the moon,
that the whole thing was staged in some Arizona desert
because *American folks are stupid that way and always will be.*
I know she had a hysterectomy and never told me.
I know that her motto was *Always be respectful of white folks.*
I know she only *thinks* she is dying soon, because it is
fashionable when you are old and black and Christian
to think so. I know that I never realized
that the way she spoke
was ever a problem
for anyone
especially her
especially me
My mother's voice:
—It's like cornbread, buttery and full of places for heat to hide.
—When she is angry, it curls into a fist and punches straight out.

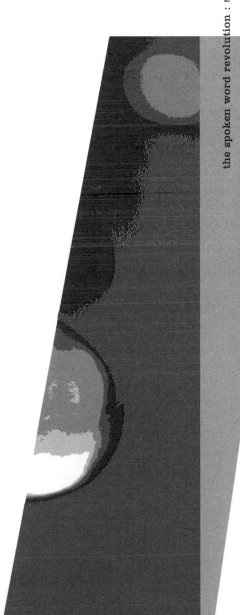

—When she is scared, it gathers strength and turns practical, matter-of-fact, like when she is calling her
    daughter to say *they found your father this morning, someone shot him and he is very dead.*
—She can't sing, not a lick, not at all. When she tries, her voice cracks and collapses and loses all
    acquaintance with a key, and every Sunday morning
it's my mother's voice that's the loudest, unleashed and creaking toward glory.
—When my mama talks, the sound of it is flat and broad and wild with unexpected flowers, like fields in
    Alabama.

—She has never been grammatically correct. Her rap is peppered with *ain't gots* and *don't have nones*
    and *I done beens* and *she be's* and *he be's* the way mine is when I'm sweet color among coloreds and
    don't have to worry about being graded. I see no shame in this. You can't do wrong in the process of
    unwrapping a dream.
Turns out now one of my mother's leftover dreams
Is to wash history from her throat, to talk like a woman
got some sense and future, to talk English instead
of talking
wrong
Yes, I am a poet, privy to the shoes of others,
but I want my mother to be my teacher
To talk to me, one colored girl to another
To warm me up with double negatives
To take me down south
And leave me there
But I pick up the phone these days
and she is on the other end,
precisely using her new mouth.
She forgets sometimes, of course, but she
is proud of what she remembers, and it hurts
me to hear her effort, the sum of all her dreams
this one dream, whizzing us back to that moment
50 years ago, on the Greyhound bus headed for
the Windy City from Alabama—
my southern mother in one seat, dead since Memphis,
and my northern mother in the seat next to herself,
lost in that mean, unreachable dream.

*

track 23

A Motherfucker Too

"...the whole band would just like have an
orgasm every time Bird or Diz would play
...Sarah Vaughan was there also, and she's
a motherfucker too."

Miles Davis

Up to you to figure out which one of 'em
we talking about. Could be any of three,
lining the babes up like dominos,
swearing they just had the love to give,
and up on stage, passing it on,
flashing it shameless, struttin' it silly,
those blowings that coulda caught fire
if fire was what they wanted.
And two of them smack slapped,
and one of them *born*
with beep beep in his blood
and even with bebopping this heavy,
it was a mess before you knew it.
Up to you to figure out
which one we talking about.
Arkansas road walking with church funk
pumping through branches and he stop

and he wail an all-night answer
the Lord don't want nothing to do with,
blue lines so funky they smelled bad.
Irrational flyer, up there so much
Gabriel post a note saying
No sidemen needed, dammit,
keep that horn in its cage.
But he blow so tender. Up baby, up,
mute like screaming through a
closed mouth. Up baby, up,
and two of them smack slapped
and one lock himself away,
riding the back of the bitch.
Strapped down on daddy's farm,
banging the walls and *shit*,
how many ways is blue?
Came out kicking, came out crazy,
and wanted nothing else but
a hungry woman after jamming.
The three of them,
Dark appetites in triple,
and one stroked it out,
one exploded,
one just got old.
The thing to remember
is the collision of Miles, Bird, and Dizzy,
all of them lost behind Miss V,
three motherfuckers in awe of another.

roger bonair-agard

track 25

how do we spell freedom—the weusi alphabeti method

I
In 1970 I learned my alphabet
for the very first time
—knew it by heart in 1971
A is for Africa
B is for Black
C is for culture and that's where it's at
my mother taught me that from the Weusi
    Alphabeti
at a time when A was for apples in a country that
    grew mangoes
and X was for xylophone when I was learning
    how to play the steelpan
black wasn't popular
or even accepted then
but I wore dashikis sent me from nigeria

super-fly suits; sky blue with the elbow patches
sent me from america
and sandals made by original rastafari before
    weed & revolution needed fertilizer to grow
my mother rocked bright saffron saris
we were phat 20 years too early and a thousand
    miles removed
my mother preached hard work
knowledge and how not to take shit
D is for Defense
E is for Economics

II

I wrote my first protest letter at the age of 3
to my grandfather
for calling me in out the front yard
spelling fuck you with an
f-o-r-k-U
put it under his pillow in the hope
it would blow up and burn his ear off at night
    wanted to get started on this revolution thing
F is for Freedom

III

G is for Guns - we gotta get some
Weusi said
evolved into 1979 and a revolution with a
    changing face
bang bang boogie to the boogie
say up jump the boogie—let's rock—yuh don't
    stop*
black folk and brand names became entwined
we re-invented dance and made wheels roll
with a limp
Cuba had just told America he was Africa in
    Angola
K is for Kings
L is for Land—we gotta get it back

so we lost Jamaica to the IMF
Grenada to the marines
and Panama to Nancy Reagan
jeri curls became high top fades, became
    gumbies, became caesars
as Michael Jackson moonwalked his way into a
    lighter shade of pale
my mother sent me to america—she said
"Go fix that..."

*from "Rappers' Delight" —Sugar Hill Gang, 1979

IV

K is for Kidnap
S is for Slavery—Weusi explained

cool became buttah became phat
—we lost our focus and our way
just at about the time
black folk outside the nation
discovered the dangers of porkso fat backs
    became phat blacks
pigtails became dredlocks
and fades faded to bald
as Michael Jordan discovered the magic of a
    fadeaway jumper
and endorsements—

X is for the niggah who's blind deaf and dumb
X him out—Weusi said
my mother told me I should re-write that
that X is for the niggah who needs to be
    re-educated
that a corporate job does not spell freedom
marry white don't mean racist flight
a democratic vote is not a revolutionary act
and as long as there's a sweatshop in Jakarta
    there is no difference
between Patrick Ewing and OJ Simpson

V
God gave Noah the rainbow sign
—said no more water; the fire next time
J is for James Baldwin—next time is now

H is for Huey
N is for Nat Turner
T is for Tubman
M is for Malcolm, Mandela, Marley & Martin got
    shot
two weeks after he told black folk to boycott
    Coca-Cola
Jesse Jackson still scared of niggaz with a
    purpose

—and someone must learn to read the signs with
    me

*

Roger Bonair-Agard

...Naming and other Christian things

At 31 I learn that Lena is short for Magdalene
    one of those enigmas of biblical lore
whore found religion
I have often questioned her motives—this love of
    Jesus Christ
this holy supplication to the son of Man

And I think about Lena my grandmother
    great big woman—skin of ashy obsidian
hair whitened by the burden of conviction
and I wonder about this business of weeping and
    foot washing;
    but I can only remember her iron hand and
    rigid schedules
her admonition on catching me daydreaming on
    the outhouse roof
—Get down off that thing boy
—You have your book to study
—What kind of man do you intend to become?!
I recall her jacking up of my equally stern
    grandfather
reminding him of the folly
of any repeated attempts to hit her
    Never does Mary Magdalene come to mind
    not in the helpless "weeping for the crucified"
    way

not in the convenient Catholic depictions
of feminine frailty of morals and spirit
   I know of a Magdalene with fight
more Joan of Arc than Maid Marion
more Sojourner Truth than damsel in distress
   and I want to tell the withering two-
     dimensional ghost
couched and crumpled at the foot of the cross
       —Get up and fight woman!
       —Wake up and live if you love him!
       —Jack up the Pontius Pilate and refuse
         surrender

at 4 I was beaten for disrespect of my
   grandfather
at 8 because I was satisfied with only a 75 in
   Math—
because she knew   having fought battles based
   purely on conviction
that she was preparing a man for the holiest of
   crucifixions
   there would be no washing of feet here
   no flimsy eruption of tears
only the austerity of a warrior
and a Puritan insistence on perfection and effort
  the creases through her aged jowls softening
only when she thought I needed to eat   to get
   strong
       —Son yuh lookin thin; come and get
         some food

a name orients one to his universe the Lakotas
   believed
a change in name meant a chance for
   improvement
for the child who was not doing well

so having learned the root of my
   grandmother's name
I cannot summon the sympathy for Mary
   Magdalene
   cannot help her weep tears of distress
only wish I could retroactivate a name change for
   her
show her my grandmother carrying 30 lb sacks of
   coffee
   dragging her swollen leg behind her
rising from her deathbed to fight her daughter's
   battles

One day if I am worthy of her expectations
I will become a man worth crucifying
and all her beatings
her lessons
her Puritanism and super-human strength
will have taught me
that surrender is not an option

On that day I expect to see
standing at the foot of whatever urban cross they
   fashion
all five-foot-ten of Lena
pointing one huge gnarled finger at me
   the shining authority of her eyes
coming from the black forest of her flesh
the white electricity of her hair
lips trembling in rage
       —Get down off that thing boy and fight!!
       —What kind of man do you intend to
         become?!

*

Beethoven

Listen
his father
made a habit
out of hitting him
see
some men drink
some men yell
some men hit their children
this man
did it all
because I guess all men
want their boys
to be geniuses

Beethoven

little boy
living in a house
where a name meant nothing
living in a house
where mercy had to be earned
through each perfect note
tumbling up through the roof
to tickle the toes of angels

whose harps
couldn't hold half the passion
that was held in the hands
of a young boy
who was hard of hearing

Beethoven

who heard
his father's anthem
every time he put finger
to ivory
it was
not good enough
so he played slowly
not good enough
so he played softly
not good enough
so he played strongly
and when he could play no more
when his fingers cramped up
into the gnarled roots of tree trunks
it was
not good enough

Beethoven

a musician
without his most precious tool
his eardrums
could no longer pound out rhythms
for the symphonies playing in his mind
he couldn't hear the audiences clapping
couldn't hear the people loving him
couldn't hear the women in the front row
    whispering

Beethoven

as they let the music
invade their nervous system
like an armada marching through
firing cannonballs
detonating every molecule in their bodies
into explosions of heavenly sensation
each note
leaving track marks
over every inch of their bodies
making them ache
for one more hit
he was an addiction
and kings/queens
it didn't matter
the man got down on his knees
for no one
but amputated the legs of his piano
so he could feel the vibrations
through the floor
the man got down on his knees
for music

and when the orchestra played his symphonies
it was the echoes of his father's anthem
repeating itself
like a brok-broken recor-brok-broken record
it was
not good enough
so they played slowly
not good enough
so they played softly
not good enough
so they played strongly
not good enough
so they tried to mock the man
make fun of the madness
by mimicking the movements
holding their bows
a quarter of an inch above the strings
not making a sound
it was

perfect

see
the deaf have an intimacy with silence
it's there in their dreams
and the musicians turned to one another
not knowing what to make of the man
trying to calculate
the distance between madness and genius
realizing that Beethoven's musical measurements
could take you to distances
reaching past the towers of Babylon
turning solar systems into symbols
that crashed together
causing comets to collide
creating crescendos that were so loud

they shook the constellations
until the stars began to fall from the sky
and it looked like the entire universe
had begun to cry

distance must be an illusion
the man must be
a genius

Beethoven

his thoughts moving at the speed of sound
transforming emotion into music
and for a moment
it was like joy
was a tangible thing
like you could touch it
like for the first time
we could watch love and hate dance together
in a waltz of such precision and beauty
that we finally understood
the history wasn't important
to know the man
all we ever had to do was

listen.

*

the youth speak

* part 6

(tracks 39–45)

introduction

Our survey of the spoken word revolution is nearing its conclusion. Hopefully, the poems presented have been lifted off of the page and flown into your hearts, or are hovering inside your unconscious minds. We have not been able to do justice to this revolution in the limited space contained between the covers of this one book and one CD. This revolution is worldwide. It would require volumes to tell the complete tale. And it is a young revolution, ever growing and dividing and sprouting up in unexpected gardens. Two young fellows in Munich, Germany, Rayl Patzak and Ko Bylanzky, have spread spoken word like a wild wonderful fever across Germany, Austria, and Switzerland. They and others like them are missionaries of a word gospel, creating hip hop/poetry shows, slams, theater productions, and even dance nights filled with poetry spun on turntables devoted to the spoken word. A young man named Lasso, the winner of the German/Swiss International slam, has conducted slam competitions in Croatia, providing the emerging democracies of eastern Europe a forum for expressing their newfound freedom. Pilot le Hot, a young French performer, is spreading the social/cultural slam movement across France. Kirill Medvedev, a young student from Moscow, recently performed on a stage erected in the Stazione Termini (the main station) of Rome, with translations of his work projected on a screen over his head as he spun his mother tongue out over the audience and into their Italian ears.

This revolution is fueled by young passionate voices that believe in the power of language. In Los Angeles in the spring of 2002, Youth Speaks, a San

Francisco based youth poetry organization with chapters in New York and Seattle that is spreading performance poetry across the country, held a benefit in an art gallery packed with high rollers. The headliner on the bill was the artist, actor, and poet Viggo Mortensen. Two hundred people were on hand to hear high school kids lay down verse more articulate and more honest than most adults could or would dare to. In D.C., the Writers Corp takes poetry into the inner city and uses it as a tool to motivate children to care about reading and writing skills. Poetry Alive, a North Carolina–based arts organization has been demonstrating the power of performance poetry in schools since the early 1980s by bringing classic American poems to life through ensemble performance. Young Chicago Authors and Youth Speaks teamed up to stage the 6th Annual Brave New Vocies Youth Poetry Slam Festival in Chicago in the spring of 2003. Twenty-four (or more) high schools and youth organizations from across the country will send poet competitors to perform to capacity crowds in the Windy City. These kids hold no punches. They press the truth of their lives into listeners' ears, and they do it with precision and polished technique.

In the best-case scenario, this youthful revolution will continue to be refreshed by new young voices as the once young grow old. Many of the poets you've heard and read in this book/CD were kids when they first found verse and spoke up, joining the throng, the choir, the heat, and expressing an idealism and hope that is ever present in the art of poetry—the sacred stirrings of the soul, the human heart's unstoppable courage, the inquisitive lust of our greedy minds. This is fire in the word, the spoken word. Young and old and always.

viggo mortensen

track 43

Weekends

Medicated limbs, lonely and greedy. Sick for
    attention, dying for
company, you're drunk for days. Overburdened,
    moss-rotted branches
heave slowly with the weak night breeze, like a
    failing heart, and
graze the stone wall.

The nurse in me won't let me leave.

Homemade illness hardens into sugar and batters
    your speech, draping
your dry white tongue over your teeth. Red
    pinholes for eyes, and
your mouth is a smudge.

Do I have to watch tomorrow afternoon while you
    keep your face

warm with the television and the maple drips on
    the lawn chairs that
flake and rust on the flooded terrace?

When you start snoring, I'll take the tray from
    your lap and tip you
over so I can look for the rest of your lunch under
    the green sofa
cushions and probably find those pills you've
    been hiding. By the time
the clouds dim and I start seeing us in the
    windows, I'll be drunk
myself and ready to wake you for dinner.

*

Hillside

We underestimate damage
done to the sky
when we allow words
to slip away
Into the clouds.

I remember making promises
to you outside. We
were watching flowers
that hadn't opened.
A bee darted, careful
not to stick to
your half-shut mouth.

*

Keepsake

Still unused
the letter opener
she got on her birthday
has become tarnished.
It lies on the sill
next to a seashell
she found in Florida
before moving west.
Before becoming a writer.
Before becoming a mother.
Her son wants to use it
as a dagger, to
wield it savagely
against monsters
streaming from toy-
cluttered corners
of his room
but he can't
reach it yet.

*

Lullaby

Can't hear.
Keep listening
to the right song
come up in a
drop
that runs
across the wall
and hangs
on the doorknob.
Sing together
across the city
squeeze a note
that stays in your fist
pulling your hair.

Matinee

After years of merging
and allowing yourself
to be assimilated
your hair and clothes
have turned brown.
Then one afternoon
you leave a theater
after taking in the
restored version of
"The Hero Returns" and
find yourself wanting to
be treated special.

*

She is willing to continue
feeding him himself; calls that
living on her own terms
safe in houses they promise
to build each other with
views on every side and
enough curtain to sleep
through it all.

*

Untitled

Wooed her like a dolphin
treats her like luna.
She blackens, tries experiencing nothing.
He looks for her
without touching, making pinpricks
in her furtive nakedness
like a hyena.

Flooded plains may remind her
of startled fish, sunken palaces
lit by moons and moons.
He does not know what she's
thinking, doesn't know what's worse:
believing she's come straight
from heaven or nowhere
at all.

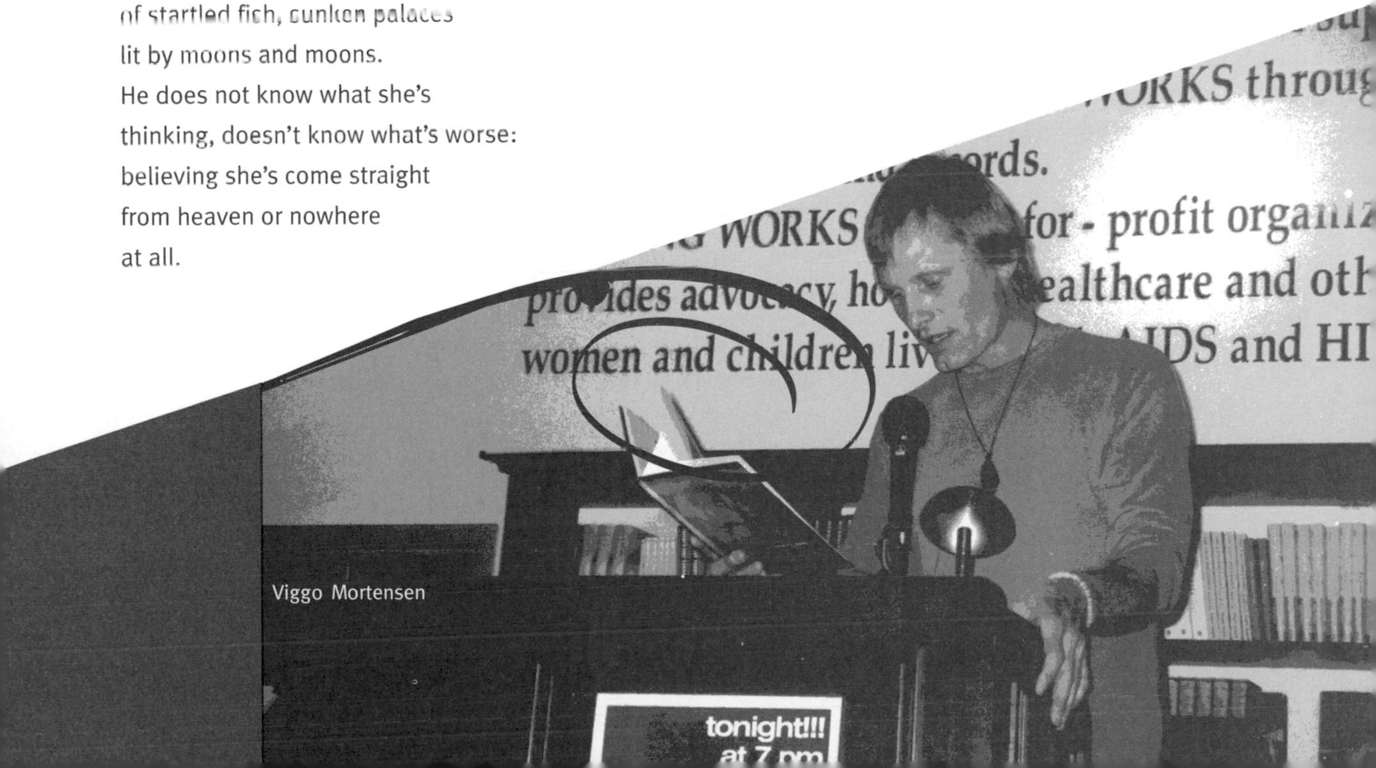

Viggo Mortensen

crossing boundaries, crossing cultures

Poetry, Performance, and the New American Revolution
(by Luis J. Rodriguez)

"The house of poetry contains many mansions."
—Owen Barfield

A number of reviewers have recently tried to tackle the phenomenal growth of performance poetry in Chicago and other parts of the country—and I don't mean just poetry slams, but the increased occasions of poetry crossing genre boundaries: poetry with music or video or theater or dance.

Today, some forty American cities sponsor poetry slams. Taos, New Mexico, is the home of the National Heavyweight Poetry Championship. And spoken word performances and multi-arts collaborations can be seen in scattered venues from New York City to Los Angeles, from Alaska to the Virginia Islands.

Because the forms are interwoven, they challenge preconceptions. They appear disconcerting, hard to compartmentalize. Still, I believe the melding of art forms, and of the poetry in bars and slams, while not taking away from the forms involved, can enrich them while finding audiences open to new ways of seeing, hearing, and being engaged.

In the April 1992 issue of Chicago's poetry magazine, *Letter eX*, an article by Jonathan Graham, "Poetry on the Rocks," attacked these same poetry events.

"Stuck in the middle of the cultural seesaw, teetering between the literati and vaudeville," wrote Graham. "Often without knowing which is which, 'performance poets' are asked to choose between being T.S. Eliot in his tweediest tweed, or an organ grinder's monkey, reciting her coincidental rendering of Shakespeare's Sonnet 36."

My biggest beef with Graham's piece was not so much with the various barbs he used to slice into the bar-and-café poetry scene—we all know some of the poems stink—but with his apparent conclusion that this is not a viable forum of expression.

Whether poetry should be done in bars, whether it should be crossed with other art forms or even used in competition is a moot point (it's happening as we speak). What I'm concerned with is the low level of critical inquiry and debate surrounding these developments. Graham's piece, for example, tended to generalize, then attack.

About two years ago, Chicago's Link Hall held a Jean Howard and Alice Q. Hargrave production of "Dancing in Your Mother's Skin" (based on her 1991 book by the same name, published by Tia Chucha Press) that included poetry, photographic images, and choreography by the Jan Bartoszek dancers. The *Chicago Reader* printed a disturbing review of the performance that essentially expressed the call for purity of form—dance is dance, poetry is poetry, photography is photography...and "never the twain shall meet!"

This is a case in point: we need critics who are open to the transfigurations, with the vision and intelligence to deal with complexities of cross-arts creation, not just knock them out of the water (for fear of the "mud").

There is a pendulum swing when it comes to discussing performance in poetry: it's either the best thing to happen to poetry or the worst. The gist of most critiques of the concept of poetry performance seems to say "good" poetry is linked to the academy, and thus to the page, while "bad" poetry is rooted in the inarticulate, illiterate masses (and often relegated to the stage).

Again, here's Gloria Klein, in another more recent article in *Letter eX* (which claims that the two poles of modern American poetry are performance poetry and academic poetry): "the performance poets are the 'sensualists without heart' and the academic poets are the 'specialists without spirit.'"

This is greatly oversimplified. There are many poets in this country (the majority, in fact) who don't fall into categories such as "performance" and "academic." And while there is much in these so-called camps that should be critiqued, there is also new and interesting poetry within them (I also know of "academic" poets quite active in performance, and vice versa).

The fact is, poetry is having a resurgence in America, and mostly from the communities and populations normally not considered poetic, such as the homeless, gang members, midwives, prisoners, carpenters, etc.

Ralph Waldo Emerson once wrote: "The language of the street is always strong…Cut these words and they would bleed; they are vascular and alive. They walk and run…a shower of bullets."

As I have often stated, young people in the South Bronx and Compton, with far fewer resources than most of us, have recreated word usage into a hip hop culture, proving the language is always alive. Too often, though, these young people are considered untalented because they lack the subtleties, the so-called gift for layered meaning. But look again—often without schooling in the language arts they seem to be more in tune with present events than most professional poets, let alone journalists.

Sometimes the "bullets" hit, sometimes they don't (I could add that perhaps the more precise they are, the more they are able to strike a target). Still, the whole concept of poetry in bars or in slams is predicated on a promise: anyone and everyone, if they want to, can do poetry.

It has long been proven by much more endowed minds than mine that the capability of creating poetry is within everyone, and should be everyone's property, not just a few. This is why I do poetry workshops among the homeless, with gang youth, among Spanish-speaking parents, in jails and migrant camps…anywhere I can. It's the social division of labor, its class nature, that concentrates artistic talent in particular individuals, and suppresses it in the majority of people.

This is often couched in terms like "some are talented and gifted, while some are not." The fact of the matter is, every human being is "gifted" for language expression, for creativity and intellectual discourse. The social division of labor only provides that a few will get the proper nurturing to develop these innate capabilities.

In addition, I believe the process of art forms meandering through and outside the genre boundaries is linked to a consciousness of cross-cultural participation. African, Latino, Native American, Asian, and European aesthetic sensibilities are swimming in the same sea we call American culture. In many of these traditions, dance told stories, songs conveyed images, and music was rife with poetry.

It appears that along with a backlash to the rise of the multiplicity of voices in American letters, there is a backlash to the blending of art forms as well.

I'm not saying that everyone who hates poetry fusion must be against cultural diversity, or that anyone has to like poetry slams; they're not for everyone. But the so-called academy is not the only place for a thriving literature—there's good and bad poetry among the "professional" bards as well.

Graham and Klein both generalized most of the performance poetry scene by dramatizing its worst aspects—for example, the few who narrow their words to insignificance, or to those who have engendered another form of elitism in bars and cafés.

Again here's Graham: "Despite their populist mission, performance poets demand their audiences listen to them, without making any particular effort to speak to any experience other than their own."

We all know this happens. But does this mean, as Graham apparently believes, that performance poetry is by its nature elitist?

Again, elitism is a result of society's division of labor. Rather than attack the forums, we should use them to play out the content of values which objectively abhors exploitation, elitism, and privilege. If Graham is saying this, I'm with him.

In fact, I agree when he says performance poetry is "a perilous art"—but this is probably true for most art. My sense of the current level of artistic alienation and exclusivity is to fight for even more expression, not less, to say more emphatically what needs to be said, to find more ways to engage our minds, our times, our ever-shifting aesthetics—not less.

This is an age of great change. The whole of society is moving from a mechanical-based productive energy system to one based on electronics. This is upturning everything that was connected to the industrial-mechanical system—including the capitalist relations in the United States and its surro-

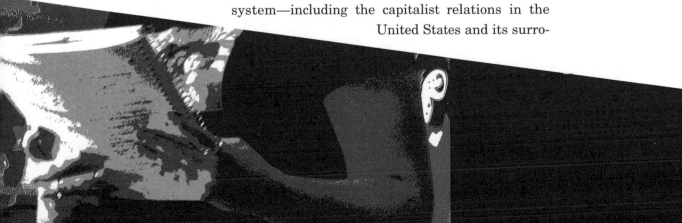

gates around the world (and, as we've seen, the bureaucracy-based, privilege-laden systems to eastern Europe).

We have not seen such tumultuous changes in some hundred years, when the mechanical-based productive energy system replaced one based on agriculture.

Then, as now, a revolution in poetics corresponded to a revolution in economics. William Sutton, in his book *American Free Verse: The Modern Revolution in Poetry* (1973, New Directions), pointed out that in the nineteenth century Wordsworth and Whitman were two poles of the "new poetics." Wordsworth expressed the changes by deliberately avoiding conventional poetic diction for "a selection of language really used by men." Whitman, a true innovator, realized in free verse the concept of organic forms, using the word "ensemble" to suggest the complexity of poetic order, and to become receptive to all kinds of experience.

"Through me forbidden voices," wrote Whitman.

And Emerson had this to say: "If there is any period one would desire to be born in, is it not the age of Revolutions; when the old and the new stand side by side and admit of being compared; when the energies of men are searched by fear and by hope; when the historic glories of the old can be compensated by the rich possibilities of the new era?"

We are living in such revolutionary times. So instead of being wary or discomforted by poetry in bars, in competition, or in homeless shelters, we should ride the tremors to a new poetics, a turning toward the common life, and to become the most indicative of what these tremors have wrought.

Why not expand the boundaries of poetic expression? Poetry in sports events. In political rallies and inaugurals. Besides on buses we need poetry on the back of cereal boxes, in between TV and cable broadcasts (not as commercials to sell things, but for the sale of the word). To expand meaningful discourse in this country.

"For it is not meters, but meter-making argument, that makes a poem," Emerson said some one hundred years ago. "A thought so passionate and alive that, like the spirit of a plant or animal, it has an architecture of its own, and adorns man."

reprinted from *Another Chicago Magazine*

Three A.M.

How many times
have I repeated his lies
to the stars
How many more do I have?
The safety I find in him
it scares me
it scares me
...so
I question him
"will you catch me when I fall?"
and so starts the game of
t r u s t
blindly letting myself fall
in
all
directions
pushing responsibility
consequence away like I've
pushed away my fears
wrapped in a package
for you
to do with what you will
as long as my face

and theirs
never meet again
so I will live my life
without guilt without conscience riding on my
        shoulder
morality whispering in my ear so I will never have
to hear
warnings from my peers
knowing they are right
that I should follow
become advice's shadow
and take the path
of safety
of assurance
and of reassurance
Let risk be forever in my feet
and danger always at my heel
let me watch the morning's sunrise
pale the night sky
through the window of my dreams of foreign
        places
evening's song
my beckoning to the waiting world

I want to feel the earth breathe beneath me
I want to wake up next to freedom
my cares tossed out the window
like old clothes
my shell yet waits to be
broken   I have yet to
stop into Earth's parade
so I go on with this charade
and fear above all

"will you
catch me when
I fall?"

*

On Rain

a drop
in sweet surrender to the greedy pull of gravity
the tiny pools fall blindly toward earth
squishing into the ground. A kamikaze mission.

a child asks her mother
"what is thunder?"
and she cannot answer so instead
tells her a story to the rhythm
of the rain tapping above them, seeking
        entrance.

Thunder is...
it is
a blanket, covering earth's face in audible
        reprimand.
like the sky above is a blanket.
it keeps you from fear.

and rain...
rain is death. No. life.
temporary and soft
falling down, down,
further and further away from the comfort
of the womb.

*

chinaka hodge

Losing

waking to bennie and lucretia skipping rocks in
   my mind
again
the shadows cast across what I remember

bennie and lucretia skipping hand
in hand
rocks in my mind again.

November '01 is draining into December.
They breathe down my back
Creased autumn crashes against the window.
The thermostat glides to stop.
Lying convex though my breasts ache.
Pillow like a mask.
The odor of this instant in my linen.

bennie and lucretia are shaking me
Awake
This is the only time they have called me
By name

I flash to my most prevalent memories
Six years old no younger. Barreling through the
   needle eyed stairway. Kicking up stucco.
greatgramma greatgramma
These were the oldest tears I'd ever seen.
She's stuck in the slip she's pulling over head
Sherlynn help
Sherlynn help
But I'm not sherlynn
Or helping
A giggle escapes

I wish I could take it back
Lying convex rattling off apologies 11 years later
For not helping
For not being sherlynn
For not swallowing the laughter
For having it in the first place
If I'd stumbled into her shattered kitchen of a
   mind
Spice rack knocked over
Broken dishes and snatches of recipes from a
   book

Without a spine
Coffee or tea
She asks then
Where is my, where is my
She cannot remember

What she does remember is this

The space between caintsee and cainstee when
    she's been
Coon wench nigra
Or the help

She remembers the shining faces of her jewish
    employers
And what it felt like at the end of her day
Chloemily, daughter, this is why we recline

She remembers those forever long drapes
That looked like elephant tusks
And how she pulled through
Every stitch
Each one love and struggle for her
    granddaughters

She remembers cooking 'til it hurt
In all of the appropriate places

But she doesn't remember me
She doesn't remember Chloe, her daughter
And all us women just float on the alzheimer's
    itself
For just a spell

Great Grand Mother
What happened 11 years ago is as fresh for me
As your memory is for you from when chloe really
    was that small
I am beginning to understand
And you are just one of my kin struggling with
    this illness

Y'all got cheated
Scrub white floors thru work week
Dip brimmed hats on Sunday
Worry storms for your sons
Dodge firehose dodge nigger dodge cotton
    thorns
Warm evening in Arkansas Bennie
Big buildings in Manhattan Lucretia
Hold men that love the shape of your calves to
    ragtime in dark
Burn fingers on ovens on crosses out front
Clutch bible clutch bible clutch bible
Live through this
And not remember

It makes me angry lying convex
But I am learning great grandmothers
Weave past to future
Cup my mother's skin
Peel this grape of a world between my teeth
While they are white and my own
And serve this purpose

But then the night flits on
And I do not remember where I left my
    grandmothers
Skipping   skipping   skipping

*

from **Guilt**

So what's the feeling you get
Riding the 22 on a cold day through the Mission
sitting comfortably in the back seats
as you cross back streets
with new beats In your ears
A gray haired grandmother
scarf loosely tied above tired eyes
waits with two impatient niños at the bus stop
she's carrying three days of groceries in her left
　　hand
and toting a wire checkered cart with the other
　　four in the right
She sits, patient, feet crossed—hands cupped in
　　lap
It's chilly out and the bus is full,
but not that full
You approach the stop as the three wait,
preparing their passes—ready to board
Driver doesn't stop, slow down, flinch, double
　　take
doesn't even care
She's behind schedule and won't take her time to
　　save another's

even for those who run along side
banging bus doors and windows
pleading, helplessly
because their feet are tired
and cars cost too much money
I feel EMPTY

What feeling do you get
hearing your father speak of two roomed houses
dust bowls and tumbleweeds rolling by
eight living there and he
just a little brown boy
getting into trouble for being just a little brown
　　boy
Fending for himself and the other five when dad
　　left town to work
and mom left home to work
gone too long
the pitter patter of the rain
on corrugated tin roofs
fifty cent army surplus shoes
soles making black tire marks because that's
　　what made them

Getting out and making himself—success
watching family, friends, kids and community die
    as he tried to save lives
and see them lived
I feel his HARDSHIP

What's the feeling you get when
your friend tells you
she whispers because she's afraid
Cries because it hurts so bad
and she just can't remember
"why would somebody do that"
under tears
under unraveled emotions and times she has to
    forget
She won't call it rape
that's a crime
a crime a victim can't commit
Your chest hurts like hers because they're
    pressed together
and you fear crying too
she doesn't want to be touched and held
doesn't want to tear again
but water still spreads between thinly laced
    eyelashes
top and bottom
I feel her PAIN

It's that feeling you get
seeing shoe shine boys
black wax on fingertips but they're not giving
    prints yet
same pair of pants from five days past
they should be in school
but the family has to eat and heating bills go up
    in the winter
men hobble on what's left of sun bathed legs
hands blister, gripping crutches too tightly
but they're alive
war torn
landmines kill children
because they're closer to the ground
Women mob to maquiladora factories
With no contract they just want to send some
    money and help the family
No break, no bathroom, sleep under the sewing
    machine, eat if you can
The biggest gang war
controversial territory and
too many children laying in streets
bullets, blasts, do it again
and
I'm watching
I'm drowning, because
I never learned to swim
I feel HELPLESS

This is
Emptiness
hardship
pain
helplessness
intrinsically meshed to where they become the
   same
GUILT
My stomach hurts
and my pulse pounds a shaking sternum
I want to help
I know I can help
I just don't know how
I've been too blessed in my life not to
I was told outward vision and knowledge was
   noble
but that's just not enough
People hurt and hunger
I complain and feast
trying to come plain with me
My water runs from faucets
not rivers but it's just as cold
chain around neck but I'm free and it's not heavy
Privileged for those who suffered before
not suffering for those who are now privileged
This hurt is nothing
this suffering is nothing
my experience is nothing to that of others
So I suffer
hurt
experience
I can't help it
I can't help
Becoming content with a condition
I can't

I just want to do something
Don't question my conscience
heart leads
not because I think I can win
but because it's the right thing to do

*

First Period

half way through first period
dust accumulated on the sweaty palm of my
    raised hand
must be a centimeter thick by now
as the chicken-legged teacher goes around the
    room
defacing students homework from last night
with red pen graffiti
that focuses more on missed commas than the
    content of the sentences

he finally decides to acknowledge me

"Mr. Derrig, why do I have a feeling that this is
    another one of your dumb
comments. You constantly waste my time. Why
    don't you just drop out or something?"

why don't I just drop out
why don't I just drop out!

and it was at that moment that all statistics
    began to make sense to me
statistics of children whose mouths water more
    for the many taste of
society corner slanged penicillins
than the cardboard textures of diplomas
with pipes more important to fill
than class requirements
statistics of classes cut
to avoid battlefields full of aggravated shrapnel
from teachers with exploding tempers
teachers with magnifying glasses at the end of
    pointers
who feed off the brightness of surrounding
    students

to singe holes in the esteems of those who need
    just a little more help
than
others

I wanted to turn my shot-down hand into a fist
I wanted to hit him 'til he was incapable of
    speaking anymore
but I didn't want to become another number in
    overflowing manila folders
of children arrested in school

and we wonder why a gun seems to fit perfectly
    in the hands of this generation's adolescents

ladies and gentlemen
I'm writing this poem to highlight that which has
    been stuck like gum
underneath wobbly desks
free from parental eyes
only to mess the hand of those who have to sit
    there
I'm writing this poem to speak for all the rows of
    children before me
who remained voiceless in the cracks of school
    and its sound proof text books

I'm writing this poem for all the children who
    have not yet been named
the ones that will one day have to fill these rows
    I've been struggling in
only to enter classrooms where they'll be shot
    down for what they feel

ladies and gentlemen
the future of America is being crushed between
    the molars
of power-hungry tyrants who think class rooms
    are boot camps

and if we have any teachers in the audience
I urge you to understand that the hand you grab
    the chalk with
the hand you grab those red pens with
the voices you speak with
are oversized chisels
and you must proceed to teach with caution
for what you say and what you do is written in
    stone
and if you chisel too hard these minds can crack

"So what don't you understand now, Mr. Derrig?"

I just wanted to know if I could go to the
    bathroom

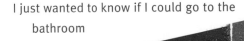

Brave New Voices

(by James Kass)

It is January 19, 2003. Tomorrow night, Youth Speaks hosts another performance. Six hundred or so will turn out to Yerba Buena Center for the Arts to listen to teen poets celebrate the Martin Luther King Jr. holiday in what's become an annual tradition here in San Francisco. It's a celebration of the best kind: a reflection on the past with an embrace of the future. It is a dream in the possible.

Through poetry, we embrace possibilities. We build new history texts. We learn about love, about pain, about war. And we invite new voices in at any given moment, and we recognize there will always be more new voices coming.

Here at Youth Speaks, we strive to give growing numbers of young people avenues in which to investigate and explore their lives as they change and develop in a changing and developing world. As educators, we give young writers as many tools as possible in order to think critically and present themselves with intention. In fact, we've made a deal with them: *if we're going to give you large public forums in which to speak*, we say, *then you have got to take responsibility for what it is you say.*

One of the projects I'm most excited by is Brave New Voices, the National Youth Poetry Slam Festival. Taking place in a different city each year since 1998, Brave New Voices brings together over two hundred young poets from all parts of the country. Through collaborations with youth advocates, nonprofit organizations, educators, poets, and youth themselves, we've been able to build an exciting annual event that continually reinvigorates itself through the addition of newer and younger voices.

Finding new ways to approach language, teenagers are fusing traditional and inherited forms with the language and rhythms of their everyday lives to get closer and closer to what it is they need to say. It is a revolution of sorts, one that is changing how young people perceive themselves and how the rest of the society receives them. Through programs like Brave New Voices, we can make sure that teenagers are able to pick up the pen and take hold of the microphone to become true cultural participants.

James Baldwin wrote that "American history is longer, larger, more beautiful, and more terrible than anything anyone has ever said about it." Like history, poetry has more to it and has been moving in more directions at all times than any of us could ever know. All we can do is continue to add to it. Move the pens across the page. Speak into the mic. Come into the open world in which we all can play a role.

Over the last eight years, I've watched thousands of youth begin writing, and seen poetry fundamentally shift in this process. I've heard young writers from throughout the country open up (or as we say in the Bay, busting) in ways that weren't available when I was a teenager. Youth from all cultural backgrounds are looking into their histories and finding generations past that have embraced the singing, writing, and sharing of poetry. Poetry readings are packed nowadays, full of highly energetic and receptive crowds. No longer packaged as an exclusive art form, poetry has become one of the truly honest ways to communicate for a whole generation hungry for just such an opportunity. For those who really engage with it, poetry becomes a way to bring breath to actions, clarity to thought, language to life, and each of us to each other.

When I was young, I was taught what poems were supposed to look and sound like, and that in order to write them I needed to step out of my everyday life—hope some magical muse would whisper something profound to me (and only me), so that I could then enter into a rarified voice and tackle *poetry*. And I learned, in that way, that poetry wasn't necessary. That maybe it was frivolous to even attempt to be a poet. After all, poetry was tucked away high up on the dusty shelves. Today's generation of poets and poetry organizations is working to change that.

As a founder of a youth-based literary arts center, I'm often asked what I think the future of poetry will bring, but I have no idea. As history progresses in an ever-changing world, so too does poetry, leaving us with no way to know what poetry will sound and look like in ten years, much less one hundred. I know what I want though: for everyone to know it's in their lives already. We just have to open up to its possibilities.

Brave New Voices is about possibilities: educational, cultural, individual, and communal. Inside Youth Speaks, we explore these possibilities—conducting writing and performance workshops with thousands of teenagers a year; scheduling visits to schools and field trips for teachers to come visit us; planning events; pressing CDs; publishing the writings of new writers through *First Word Press*—all while working with an incredible group of poets and teachers who want to revitalize the way language is taught in the classroom by giving youth access to what is buried just beneath their tongues. Almost every day a new poet comes through our door, looking for a place to write and a community to write with. The individual voice is growing, finding its place in a larger world, sharing in the exciting energy of a newborn poem.

Each year too, audiences for poetry grow. In San Francisco, it is common for more than a thousand people to come out on a Saturday night to listen to the Youth Speaks poets. Brave New Voices consistently packs houses from coast to coast. And even if none of these audience members ever pick up a pen, each will know a little something more about poetry than before they came in through that door. This is the future. Poetry as a place where all are welcome. Look around, I say now. Just look around and listen. This is where poetry is going, to a place where it's necessary. And to a place where it's fun.

epilogue

There were three bums sitting outside the door, panhandling for change. And the man with the dark black coat and ponytail carefully climbed over them, bag on shoulder, dropping some dimes on their lap as he walked in the bar.

Opening the door revealed the dive in all of its agony. The small, damp, narrow bar reeked. Album covers of old "one hit wonder" jazz bands were pinned to the spider-cracked black walls. The man shuffled in, kicking the gray Chicago used-to-be Bucktown snow, trying to avoid other puddles. Most of the puddles came in with the old vets and neighborhood rummies, he hoped. Throwing his bag over his head as he marched forward to a small step-stage, he was careful to avoid the leaking ceiling. A brown, smelly liquid creeped out of the middle of the ceiling and carried along the wall. Those observant enough to see through the dark haze of smoke guessed it was coming down from the upstairs toilet. The man just ignored it and headed to the stage, dropping his coat and bag on a table. After all, despite its appearance, it was rumored that both Studs Terkel and Jimmy Carter had occasioned the Get Me High. And it was the home to the hottest poetry reading in town and the grassroots movement later to become slam—it was just that nobody knew it yet.

"Hey, you want anything?" yelled the crumply, lived-in bartender. Over the towel on his shoulder, the calendar that read 1985 was stained yellow from cigarette smoke.

"No thanks, Butchy, let's get the show started."

And with that, the man dressed in black with the long graying ponytail jumped on the edge of the stage and screamed with a contorted smile and devilish rage, "What's the use in being so proud, when the things that change shouldn't, and the things that should, stay fixed in the blind imbalance of Liberty…" while his body transformed to new shapes of expression. As he leaped off the stage to fulfill the conclusion of his poem, the audience stared in wonder. The wordman stepped back up on stage and said: "My name's Marc Smith!" And the watchful crowd responded, "So what!"

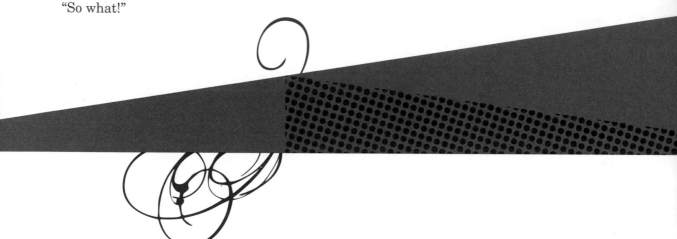

About the editors

Mark Eleveld is copublisher at EM Press and a board member of the Midland Authors Society in Chicago. He is a freelance writer and book reviewer for the *Kankakee Daily Journal* in Illinois. Mark Eleveld did press relations for poet Marc Smith from 1993 to 1996. He teaches English at Joliet West High School and is a philosophy instructor at the University of St. Francis in Illinois. He lives in Joliet, Illinois.

Few people can say that they single-handedly created a whole new art form. **Marc Smith** is one of those people. Since Marc began the Poetry Slam in 1987, competitive performance poetry has spread throughout the world. Through his creation of the Uptown Poetry Slam and many poetry organizations and ensembles such as the Pong Unit One, the Bob Shakespeare Band, Neutral Turf's Chicago Poetry Festival and the Poetic Theatre Project, Marc has influenced and inspired poets to shake off the notion that poetry belongs only to the high-minded. Author of *Crowdpleasers*, Marc has performed poetry to more than one hundred thousand people during his sixteen-year-strong weekly show at the Green Mill Lounge in Chicago. He lives in Chicago.

Contributor Biographies

Todd Alcott was born in 1961, and grew up in the northwest suburbs of Chicago. In the 1980s, he moved to New York to pursue a career as a playwright. He performed his monologues at many different downtown venues, culminating in the solo show *Living in Flames* at the Public and the John Houseman Theater. In recent years, he has split his time between staging his plays in downtown spaces and writing screenplays for Hollywood. Plays include *High Strangeness*, *The Users Waltz*, *Tulpa*, *A Pound of Flesh,* and *Helsinor*. He coauthored the animated film *Antz*.

Sherman Alexie, a Spokane/Coeur d'Alene Indian, was born in 1966 on the Spokane Indian Reservation in Wellpinit, Washington. He received his BA in American studies from Washington State University in Pullman. His books of poetry include *One Stick Song* (Hanging Loose, 2000), *The Man Who Loves Salmon* (1998), *The Summer of Black Widows* (1996), *Water Flowing Home* (1995), *Old Shirts & New Skins* (1993), *First Indian on the Moon* (1993), *I Would Steal Horses* (1992), and *The Business of Fancydancing* (1992). He is also the author of several novels and collections of short fiction including *The Toughest Indian in the World* (Atlantic Monthly Press, 2000); *Indian Killer* (1996); *Reservation Blues* (1994), which won the Before Columbus Foundation's American Book Award; and *The Lone Ranger and Tonto Fistfight in Heaven* (1993), which received a Hemingway Foundation/PEN Award. Among his other honors and awards are poetry fellowships from the Washington State Arts Commission and the National Endowment for the Arts and a Lila Wallace-Reader's Digest Writers' Award. Alexie and Chris Eyre wrote the screenplay for the movie *Smoke Signals*, which was based on Alexie's short story "This Is What it Means to Say Phoenix, Arizona." The movie won two awards at the Sundance Film Festival in 1998 and was released internationally by Miramax Films. He is also a three-time World Heavyweight Poetry Champion. Alexie lives with his wife and son in Seattle, Washington.

Poet, performance artist, and novelist **Paul Beatty** was born in 1962 in West Los Angeles. He received an MFA in Creative Writing from Brooklyn College and an MA in Psychology from Boston University. His books of poetry include *Joker, Joker, Deuce* (Penguin, 1994) and *Big Bank Take Little Bank* (1991).

He is also the author of the novels *Tuff* (2000) and *The White Boy Shuffle* (1996). Paul Beatty lives and works in New York City.

Marvin Bell lives in Iowa City, Iowa. The most recent of his seventeen books is *Nightworks: Poems 1962–2000*. He is a longtime faculty member at the Writers' Workshop at the University of Iowa, and the State of Iowa's first Poet Laureate. His writing has been called "ambitious without pretension," and he himself has been referred to in print as "a maverick" and "an insider who thinks like an outsider."

After winning Guild Complex's 1999 Gwendolyn Brooks Open Mic award, **Tara Betts** published her collection of poems, *Can I Hang?* She also represented Chicago as a slam team member at the 1999 and 2000 National Poetry Slams. She has performed her work at the Museum of Contemporary Art, Womanmade Gallery, the Metro, the Field Museum of Natural History, Chicago Cultural Center, and several colleges, universities, and Chicago public and alternative schools. She has shared the stage with Patricia Smith, Rosellen Brown, Afaa Michael Weaver, Kwame Dawes, and Grammy nominee Jill Scott. Tara's work has appeared in the Steppenwolf Theater production *Words on Fire*, *Obsidian III*, *Columbia Poetry Review*, *These Hands I Know* (Sarabande, 2002); *That Takes Ovaries!* (Three Rivers Press/Crown, 2002); *Role Call* (Third World Press, February 2002); *Bum Rush the Page: A Def Poetry Jam* (Three Rivers Press/Crown, 2001); *Poetry Slam: The Competitive Art of Performance Poetry* (Manic D Press, 2000), and *Power Lines: A Decade of Poetry from Chicago's Guild Complex* (Tia Chucha Press, 1999).

Roger Bonair-Agard is a native of Trinidad and Tobago. He is coauthor of *Burning Down the House* from Soft Skull Press and has appeared in several anthologies. In 1998, he was named Nuyorican Poets Café "Fresh Poet of the Year" and also won the team National Poetry Slam that same year. In 1999, he was the Individual National Slam Champion. Roger has completed several teaching residencies in high schools and colleges across the country and has appeared on the *MacNeil/Lehrer News Hour*, HBO's *Def Poetry Jam*, and *60 Minutes* on CBS. When traveling, Roger keeps his belongings in Brooklyn.

Michael R. Brown, author of *Falling Wallendas* (Tia Chucha, 1994), has two new books of poetry *Susquehanna* (Ragged Sky, 2002) and *The Man Who Makes Amusement Rides* (Hanover Press, 2003). He has published his poetry, fiction, travel articles, and columns in wide-ranging periodicals all over the world. He holds a PhD in English and education from the University of Michigan, where he studied with Robert Hayden. For forty years, he has taught at high schools and universities from the South Side of Chicago to South Korea. Currently, he is Professor of Communications at Mount Ida College where, in 1999, he won the first Ronald J. Lettieri Award for Teaching Excellence. Brown was a finalist in the 1991 individual competition of the U.S. National Poetry Slam. In 1992, he organized the national slam, and he was on the Boston slam teams that won the National Championship in 1993 and finished fourth in 1995. He won the open slam at the 2000 Provincetown Poetry Festival, and he was the hit of the 2001 Rockland (New York) Jazz and Blues Festival. He has performed his poems from Jerusalem to Taipei and Vancouver to Key West. Every Wednesday night, he hosts the Boston slam at the Cantab Lounge, Cambridge, Massachusetts. Michael Brown is co-producer of the Culture of Peace, an exhibit of art and poetry to further the U.N. mandate for a decade of the Culture of Peace. He is general secretary of the Poetry Olympics, first held in Stockholm in 1998. He is webmaster for www.slamnews.com.

Lisa Buscani is a National Poetry Slam Champion and the author of *Jangle* (Tia Chucha Press) as well as two critically and popularly acclaimed solo shows, *Carnivale Animale* and *At That Time*. She is currently playing in *Late Night Catechism*.

Regie Cabico is coeditor of *Poetry Nation: A North American Anthology of Fusion Poetry* (Vehicule Press, Montreal). He is a member of the poetry slam team Mouth Almighty, which won first place at the 1997 National Slam. His work has appeared in more than thirty anthologies, including the *Outlaw Bible of American Poetry* (Thunder's Mouth Press, 1999.)

Andrei Codrescu is a regular commentator on National Public Radio and has written and starred in the Peabody Award–winning movie *Road Scholar*. He is MacCurdy Distinguished Professor of English and Comparative Literature at Louisiana State University in Baton Rouge, Louisiana, where he edits *Exquisite Corpse: a Journal of Letters & Life* (www.exquisitecorpse.org). He is also a poet, novelist, and essayist, whose books include: *Casanova in Bohemia* (2002); *Alien Candor: Selected Poems 1970–1997*; *The Blood Countess* (1995); *Messiah* (1999); *The Hole in the Flag: A Romanian Exile's Story of Return and Revolution; Ay, Cuba: A Socio-Erotic Journey;* and *Hail, Babylon: In Search of the American City at the End of the Millennium*.

Billy Collins has published six collections of poetry, including *Questions About Angels*, *The Art of Drowning*, and *Picnic, Lightning*. In May 2001, Picador in the UK published his collection of poems, *Taking Off Emily Dickinson's Clothes*. In June 2001, Billy Collins was appointed U.S. Poet Laureate 2001–2003. In fall 2002, Random House published his latest collection of poems, *Nine Horses*. He is professor of English at Lehman College of the City University of New York and lives in Somers, New York.

Kevin Coval, poet, MC, essayist, activist, and educator, has performed extensively, nationally and internationally from Cape Town, South Africa, at The Parliament of the World's Religions, to Bombay, India, and Ocho Rios, Jamaica. A Writing Fellow at National-Louis University and Poet-in-Residence at the Cook County Juvenile Detention Center, Kevin was featured in January 2002 on Russell Simmons's HBO *Def Poetry Jam*, and was a member of the 2002 National Poetry Slam Team for Chicago. He has shared a stage with Cornel West and Amiri Baraka, opened for Ani DiFranco, closed for Ntozake Shange, got down with jazz legends Kahil El' Zabar and Ernest Dawkins, and blessed mics with MCs Bahamadia and Medusa. Kevin teaches and creates workshops for Young Chicago Authors, Guild Complex, and the University of Hip Hop to help facilitate the growing youth writing community in the city of Chicago.

DJ Renegade (Joel Dias-Porter) was born and raised in Pittsburgh, Pennsylvania. He is of Cape Verdean descent on his mother's side (Fogo). After high school, he enlisted in the U.S. Air Force. After being kicked out of the service, he became a professional disc jockey in the D.C. area. In 1991, he quit his job and began living in homeless shelters, while undergoing an extensive Afrocentric study program. In 1994–1998 he competed in the National Poetry Slam finishing fifth, fourth, third, and second in the individual competition, and he is the 1998 and 1999 Haiku Slam Champion. His poems have been published in *Time* magazine, the *Washington Post, Callaloo, Obsidian II, Underwood Review, Paterson Literary Review, Asheville Poetry Review, Red Brick Review, the GW Review*, and in anthologies *Meow: Spoken Word from the Black Cat, 360 Degrees of Black Poetry, Slam (The Book), Revival: Spoken Word from Lollapalooza, Poetry*

Nation, *Beyond the Frontier*, *Catch a Fire*, and *The Black Rooster Social Inn: Poetry and Art of the Black Rooster Collective*, which he also edited. In 1995, he received the Furious Flower "Emerging Poet Award." He has performed his work on the *Today* show, in a commercial for Legal Jeans, in the documentaries *Voices Against Violence* and *SlamNation*, on BET's *Teen Summit* and *By the Book*, and in the feature film *Slam* which won the Grand Jury Prize at the Sundance Film Festival in 1998. Currently, he is a part-time teacher at Duke Ellington School of the Arts and at work on a book of poems about the Cape Verdean-American experience. A CD of jazz and poetry titled *A Desperate Wrestling of Tongues* is also in the works. He is a graduate of the Cave Canem Workshop and informally educated.

Kent Foreman is a veteran actor, performance poet, lyricist, and occasional screenwriter whose poetry has been featured in two professional stage productions directed by his mentor, Oscar Brown Jr. He has toured as a jazz poet with Max Roach, and performed with Amiri Baraka, Maya Angelou, and Allen Ginsberg, among others. He has won the Chicago Historical Society's esteemed Carl Sandburg Award and is an acknowledged slam champion in Chicago, having appeared on the 1998 Bellwood (Illinois) team, and the 2000 and 2002 Green Mill teams.

Regie Gibson has performed, taught, and lectured at schools, universities, theaters, and various other venues on two continents and in seven countries, most recently in Havana, Cuba. Regie and his work appear in the New Line Cinema film *love jones*, based largely on events in his life. The poem titled "Brother to the Night (A Blues for Nina)" appears on the movie soundtrack and is performed by the film's star, Larenz Tate. Regie performed "Hey Nappyhead" in the film with world renowned percussionist and composer Kahil El Zabar. Regie has performed at the Art Institute of Chicago, Chicago's Museum of Contemporary Art, Chicago Field Museum of Natural History, Chicago Cultural Center, Elgin Symphony Orchestra Hall with the Elgin Symphony Orchestra, Symphony Center with the members of the Chicago Symphony Orchestra at the Day of Art Festival, the Steppenwolf Theatre's award-winning Traffic Series with David Amram, Harvard University's Longfellow Hall for the Cambridge Poetry Festival, and the Rock and Roll Hall of Fame in Cleveland, Ohio. Regie is the 1998 National Poetry Slam Individual Champion, was selected one of *Chicago Tribune's* Artist of the Year for Excellence (1998) for his poetry, judged the *Chicago Sun-Times* 2001 Poetry Competition with Marc Smith and Mark Strand (University of Chicago professor and 1999 Pulitzer Prize winner for poetry), and is regularly featured on National Public Radio. Regie is widely published in magazines, journals, and anthologies, such as *Power Lines: An Anthology of Poetry,* along with three Pulitzer Prize–winning poets: Gwendolyn Brooks, Yosef Komunyakaa, and Lisel Mueller. His first full-length book of poetry *Storms Beneath The Skin* (EM Press) was released in 2001.

Celena Glenn is a ballet-toed bulldozer shoveling blankets off of the ice-covered lakes of our hearts' malfunctions. Former host at the Nuyorican Poets Café and twice on the national poetry slam championship team, she is featured in *Urban Scribes*, a documentary about the lives of contemporary poets, and has performed at universities across the country including Princeton, the University of California, and New York University. Celena has been featured in *Serum*, a Swedish poetry publication, *UNTOLD*, a London-based culture magazine, and *Composite*, a fashion magazine out of Japan. She recently released *Fidel con Pollo,* the paramount presentation of Gettysburgesque athletic apparel and a multimedia performance with clothing designed "for the colonialist in you" with teams like "chicken" with their captain, Colin Powell, and team "terrorist" with captain Tammy Faye.

Gregory Harms is an artist, graphic designer, and freelance writer living in Chicago. He studied philosophy at Lewis University and design at the Art Institute of Chicago. Harms is currently working on his first book, an introduction to the Palestinian–Israeli conflict. He has visited the Middle East and has lectured on the conflict and international affairs.

Edward Hirsch, a 1998 MacArthur Fellow, has published five books of poems: *For the Sleepwalkers* (1981), *Wild Gratitude* (1986), which won the National Book Critics Circle Award, *The Night Parade* (1989), *Earthly Measures* (1994), and *On Love* (1998). His new book, *Lay Back the Darkness* was published in March 2003. He has also published three prose books: *How to Read a Poem and Fall in Love with Poetry* (1999), a national bestseller; *Responsive Reading* (1999); and *The Demon and the Angel: Searching for the Source of Artistic Inspiration* (2002). He writes a weekly column on poetry for the *Washington Post Book World* and serves as President of the John Simon Guggenheim Memorial Foundation.

Chinaka Aziza Hodge is an African American womangirl who likes to write. Her work has been featured on HBO's *Def Poetry Jam*, in *Newsweek*, and on both volumes of Youth Speaks' anthology CD, *Bringing the Noise*. Currently she is Outreach Coordinator for Youth Speaks New York. Chinaka attends New York University and is studying English and education.

Recently dubbed a member of the "Poetry Pantheon" by the *New York Times* magazine and featured in a Henry Louis Gates Jr. profile in the *New Yorker*, **Bob Holman** has previously been crowned "Ringmaster of the Spoken Word" (*New York Daily News),* "Poetry Czar" (*Village Voice*), and "Dean of the Scene" (*Seventeen*). The series he produced for PBS, *The United States of Poetry*, features more than sixty poets including Derek Walcott, Rita Dove, Czeslaw Milosz, Lou Reed, and former President Jimmy Carter, as well as rappers, cowboy poets, American Sign Language poets, and Slammers. *USOP* lives on as an anthology from Harry Abrams Publishers (in its second printing), a home video from KQED, and soundtrack CD from Mouth Almighty/Mercury Records, a label Holman cofounded. He has appeared widely on TV, featured on such programs as *Nightline, Good Morning America, ABC News Magazine*, MTV's *Spoken Word Unplugged*, and *The Charlie Rose Show*, among others. The NEA has announced major preproduction support for his new poetry media project, *The World of Poetry* (worldofpoetry.org), the world's first digital poetry anthology. He is guide for Poetry on About.com (poetry.about.com), consistently a banner site with six thousand "Museletter" subscribers and thirty-five thousand hits a week. Holman's first CD, *In With The Out Crowd*, was produced by needle-drop wizard Hal Willner. Holman's latest collection of poems, *The Collect Call of the Wild*, published by Henry Holt, was proclaimed "the first poetic drop-kick into the new millennium" by *Next* magazine and "Impressive (to say the least)" by Robert Creeley—it is Holman's fifth book. He coedited *Aloud! Voices from the Nuyorican Poets Café* (also from Holt), winner of the American Book Award, having helped reopen the Café in 1989, where he ran the infamous poetry slams through 1996. Bob fronts poetry into daily life by all means: he won three Emmys over six seasons producing *Poetry Spots* for WNYC-TV, received a Bessie Performance Award, has twice been Featured Artist at the Chicago Poetry Video Festival and won International Public Television Awards for *USOP* and *Words in Your Face*, a production of the PBS series *Alive TV.* Holman was founding editor of the NYC Poetry Calendar in 1977, and has curated reading series at St. Marks Church (he worked at the Poetry Project for seven years), the Whitney Museum, the Public Theater, and other locales. He has toured the world with his "amazing traveling word show," and is Artistic Director of the touring company Real Live Poetry (washingtonsquarearts.com). He is currently Visiting Professor of Writing and Integrated

Arts at Bard College, where he adapted and directed John Ashbery's book-length poem "Girls on the Run" in spring 2001, and *Sudden Ekphrasis! The Poetry of Robert Kelly* in fall 2001. San Francisco's *Poetry Flash* says he is "his generation's Ezra Pound." He is currently the proprietor of The Bowery Poetry Club, a cafe/bar/performance space that is the first step toward his dream of a poetry-technology lab: Bowery Arts & Science.

Born and raised in Salt Lake City, Utah, **Jean Howard** moved to Chicago in 1979. Her poetry has appeared in *Harper's* magazine, the *Chicago Tribune*, *ACM*, and more than twenty literary publications. Featured on national and cable television and radio, she has combined her poetry with theater, art, dance, and photography. A participant in the original development of the Green Mill's Uptown Poetry Slam, she has won grants from the Illinois Arts Council and City of Chicago Department of Cultural Affairs. She is the author of *Dancing in Your Mother's Skin* (Tia Chucha Press).

Terry Jacobus received his degree in secondary education at Northeastern Illinois University. He studied with Gwendolyn Brooks, Edward Dorn, Ted Berrigan, and Tom Raworth in the university's creative writing program. Jacobus is the author of three books, *The Simple Ballad*, a four-part performed narrative; *Fine*, a collection of poems; and *The Poet Never Loses His Girl*, a collection of short stories. He is currently working on a new book of poetry titled *The Book of God*. He was Chicago correspondent for *Rolling Stock Magazine* from 1980–1990, poetry editor of *Strong Coffee Magazine* from 1992–1997, and was the First World Heavyweight Champion in Taos, when he defeated Gregory Corso in 1982.

Michael Kadela was born on the east side of Joliet, Illinois, in 1971, after which he immediately began the practice of causing problems for all those with whom he came into direct or indirect contact. After leaving DePaul University prior to graduation in 1991, he held a series of terribly odd jobs ranging from the cleaning of dead chickens to the scouting of movie locations for the film industry. In 2000, he represented the Green Mill Lounge at the National Poetry Slam in Providence, Rhode Island. He currently resides in Chicago.

Yusef Komunyakaa was born in Bogalusa, Louisiana, in 1947. His eleven books of poems include *Neon Vernacular: New and Selected Poems*, for which he received the Pulitzer Prize. He is a professor in the Creative Writing Program at Princeton University.

Shane Koyczan hails from Vancouver, British Columbia, and tours extensively throughout North America performing poetry. At the 2000 National Poetry Slam in Providence, Rhode Island, he won the individual championship, becoming the first international poet to do so (as well as the youngest). Shane has won the Leonard Cohen Award for Best Song, the James Ellroy Award for Best Poetic Voice, and the W.B. Yeats Award for Best Poem. He opened for Maya Angelou in San Francisco and for Saul Williams in Denmark.

Thomas Lux teaches at Sarah Lawrence College and in the Warren Wilson MFA Program for Writers. He divides his time between New York City and the Boston area. His books of poetry include *The Street of Clocks* (Houghton Mifflin, 2001); *New and Selected Poems, 1975–1995* (1997), which was a finalist for the 1998 Lenore Marshall Poetry Prize; *The Blind Swimmer: Selected Early Poems, 1970–1975* (1996); *Split Horizon* (1994), for which he received the Kingsley Tufts Poetry Award; *Pecked to Death by Swans* (1993); *A Boat in the Forest* (1992); *The Drowned River: New Poems* (1990); *Half Promised Land* (1986); *Tarantulas on the Lifebuoy* (1983); *Massachusetts* (1981); *Like a Wide Anvil from the Moon the Light*

(1980); *Sunday* (1979); *Madrigal on the Way Home* (1977); *The Glassblower's Breath* (1976); *Memory's Handgrenade* (1972); and *The Land Sighted* (1970). Thomas Lux also has edited *The Sanity of Earth and Grass* (1994, with Jane Cooper and Sylvia Winner) and has translated *Versions of Campana* (1977).

Sarah Maehl is currently studying writing at Beloit College in Wisconsin. A graduate of Beecher High School in Illinois, Sarah has already studied with novelist Clint McCown, and Noble Prize nominee poet Bei Dao. In the summer of 2000, Sarah was allowed entrance into the Prism Writing Program for Young Adults run by the Guild Complex and taught by Luis Rodriquez. In her young life, she has shared the stage with Marc Smith, Regie Gibson, Li-Young Lee, and Roger Bonair-Agard. Her poem "On rain" was published in the *Kankakee Daily Journal* in the summer of 2002.

Taylor Mali is known to the poetry slam community as the original "Score Creep." A clever strategist, he has taken a poetry slam team to the finals of the national poetry slam championship six times. For more information, visit www.taylormali.com.

Steve Marsh is the first executive director of Poetry Slam, Inc. He has been a Slammer in Ann Arbor (but not *in* the slammer in Ann Arbor) since 1988. He was a member of Ann Arbor's Slam team in Chicago in 1991, in Boston in 1992 (where Ann Arbor finished third to Boston and San Francisco), in San Francisco in 1993, in Portland in 1996, and in Austin in 1998. He cohosted the 1995 National Poetry Slam in Ann Arbor and was a central figure in the move to incorporate Poetry Slam as a nonprofit corporation in 1997. He participated in the SlamAmerica bus tour as tour manager for several days in 2000 and is the author of four chapbooks.

Jack McCarthy calls himself a "standup poetry guy." He's been on two national slam teams and has brought out two books of poetry. He's an engaging minor character in the film *SlamNation* and was a semifinalist for the Individual Slam Championship in 2000. He has been called a "legend" on the Boston scene. The *Boston Phoenix* has named him "Best Standup Poet," the Boston Poetry Awards "Best Love Poet (Male)," and the Cambridge Poetry Awards "Best Spoken Word (Male)" and "Best Humorous Poet (Male)." *The Boston Globe* says, "In the poetry world, he's a rock star."

Jeffrey McDaniel is an acclaimed performance poet whose work has appeared in many literary publications, including *Ploughshares* and *Best American Poetry 1994*. He has performed in such diverse festivals as Lollapalooza 1994, the Moscow Writers Union, the Globe in Prague, the National Poetry Slam, and at numerous venues throughout the U.S. He is the author of the books *Alibi School* and *The Forgiveness Parade*, and most recently *The Splinter Factory* (Manic D Press).

Born in Cumberland, Maryland, on April 27, 1959, **George David Miller** received a BS in Philosophy and English from Towson University in 1981, an MA from Ohio University in 1984, and a PhD in Philosophy from DePaul University in 1988. He is the author of five philosophy texts, including *Global Ethical Options* (Weatherhill) and *Peace, Value, and Wisdom: The Educational Philosophy of Daisaku Ikeda* (Rodopi). *Children of Kosen-Rufu* is his first book of poetry. In 1997, the Carnegie Foundation honored him as Illinois Teacher of the Year. He serves as editor of the Daisaku Ikeda Studies Special Series and Philosophy of Education Special Series for the Value Inquiry Book Series. Founder of the Scholars Academy of Lewis University, Miller teaches philosophy at Lewis University in Romeoville.

Brenda Moossy, a first-generation American of Lebanese descent, was born and raised in East Texas during the '50s and '60s. She has lived most of her adult life in Fayetteville, Arkansas. Now a nurse specializing in HIV, she feels her work has impacted her worldview and her writing. She is a founding and active member of the Ozark Poetry Collective, which has grown to become the Ozark Poets and Writers Collective. Brenda has four limited-edition chapbooks, and co-produced an audio tape titled *Ozark Women Poets—Snake Dreams*. She has given numerous public readings, including appearances at the Cantab Lounge in Boston, the Nuyorican Poets Café and The Knitting Factory in New York City, City Lights Bookstore in San Francisco, and Cody's Books Poetry Flash Reading Series in Berkeley. A member of the Ozarks Team to the 1995 National Poetry Slam, Brenda has also conducted classes and workshops on the craft of poetry to young writers in the Arkansas and New Jersey schools.

Viggo Mortensen, poet, artist, actor, and longtime denizen of the Venice, California, poetry scene, is the author of three poetry collections, *Ten Last Night*, *Recent Forgeries*, and *Coincidence of Memory*. In 2002, Mortensen founded Perceval Press, an independent publishing company dedicated to art, poetry, autopsies, and other hard sells. A collection of his newer poems will be published in the spring of 2003.

Only Marc Smith has been at the Uptown Poetry Slam more than Dr. Richard Prince, who has been at the Green Mill almost every Sunday night since January 1988. Prince was born and raised on the South Side of Chicago. He attended Calvin College in Grand Rapids and earned his MA at the University of Chicago and his doctorate at the University of Michigan. He has been teaching in the English Department at Lewis University for nearly thirty years. His long-standing interest in slam poetry is unusual given he never performs; however, as he explains, "A Sunday night at the Mill is part church, part school in the best sense, part social, and part connecting with authentic voices from the Chicago I know and love. And my job is to be a good audience for whatever poetry comes my way."

A three-time Los Angeles Grand Slam winner and two-time National Slam finalist, Jerry Quickley is the editor of the anthology, *Juke Joint Magic* (Juke Joint Still Press, 1998), and has written for *Time* magazine, the *Los Angeles Times*, *LA Weekly*, and *The Village Voice*. Quickley also performs on the CD, *UnBound* (Nu Groove, 2000) with Chuck D, Saul Williams, and other hip hop and spoken word artists. Off the page and in the community, Quickley is the resident poet at 33⅓, the weekly gathering of the Soul/Hip Hop/Spoken Word tribe in Los Angeles, and runs a Poetry in the Prisons workshop, helping the city's incarcerated youth craft their stories into poetry.

Peter Rabbit is the tireless promoter of the Taos Poetry Circus. He studied poetry with Charles Olson at Black Mountain College, performed at the legendary Five Spot in New York, and has performed with jazz ensembles since the mid-1950s. He has been a hipster, beatnik, hippie, and was a founding member of several intentional communities in the '60s. With wife Anne MacNaughton, he began the Taos Poetry Circus in 1982. Unpretentious and accessible, Mr. Rabbit has been on the cutting edge of the poetry scene all his life. He has six books of poetry, fiction, and nonfiction to his credit.

Luis J. Rodriguez has eight nationally published books and has won a Poetry Center Book Award, a PEN Josephine Miles Literary Award, and *Foreword* magazine's Silver Book Award, among others. His two children's books have won a Patterson Young Adult Book Award, two "Skipping Stones" Honor

Awards, and a Parent's Choice Book Award. Luis is best known for his 1993 memoir of gang life, *Always Running: La Vida Loca, Gang Days in L.A.* An international bestseller, the memoir also garnered a Carl Sandburg Literary Award, a *Chicago Sun-Times* Book Award, and was designated a *New York Times* Notable Book. He has received a Sundance Institute Art Writers Fellowship, a Lila Wallace–Reader's Digest Writers Award, a Lannan Fellowship for Poetry, an Hispanic Heritage Award for Literature, a National Association for Poetry Therapy Public Service Award, a California Arts Council Fellowship, an Illinois Author of the Year Award, several Illinois Arts Council fellowships, the 2001 Premio Fronterizo, and the "Unsung Heroes of Compassion" Award, presented by the Dalai Lama. Luis is also known for helping start a number of prominent organizations, such as Chicago's Guild Complex, one of the largest literary arts organizations in the Midwest, and its publishing wing, Tia Chucha Press, and most recently he is a cofounder of Tia Chucha's Café Cultural—a bookstore, coffee shop, performance space, art gallery, and computer center that opened in Northeast San Fernando Valley.

Cin Salach is a multimedia poet who has been performing her work around the country since 1987. A member of the first National Slam Champion Team, Cin was chosen in 1989 to be a cultural ambassador to Prague, Czech Republic. A participant in the women's performance festival Big Goddess Pow Wow since 1990, she is also the cofounder of the Loofah Method, a multimedia ensemble of spoken word, poetry, percussion, and theater, and Betty's Mouth, poetry choreographed for two voices. Her first book of poetry is titled *Looking for a Soft Place to Land.*

Beau Sia is the author of *A Night Without Armor II: The Revenge* (MouthAlmighty Books). He has two spoken word albums, *Attack! Attack! Go!* and *Dope and Wack*, and is featured in the films *Slam* and *SlamNation*. He is a member of two national poetry slam championship teams and has appeared on all seasons of HBO's *Russell Simmons Presents Def Poetry*. He has also performed on ESPN's *2000 Winter X-Games*, *Showtime! at The Apollo*, and the *2003 Tony Awards*. He is an original cast member of *Russell Simmons' Def Poetry Jam on Broadway* and is currently on national tour with the production. His home base is www.beausia.com and he does what he wants.

Patricia Smith, a poet, performance artist, and journalist, was born in 1955. Her volumes of poetry include *Close to Death* (Zoland Books, 1993); *Big Towns, Big Talk* (1992), which won the Carl Sandburg Literary Award; and *Life According to Motown* (1991). Her latest work of nonfiction, *Africans in America*, is a companion volume to the PBS series. Her poems have been anthologized in *Unsettling America: An Anthology of Contemporary Multicultural Poetry* (1994) and *Aloud: Voices from the Nuyorican Poets Cafe* (1995). A four-time individual champion of the National Poetry Slam, Smith has performed her work around the world. She has also written and performed two one-woman plays, one of which was produced by Derek Walcott's Trinidad Theater Workshop in the spring of 1994. An audiocassette of Smith performing before a live audience, *Always in the Head*, includes selections from her first three books. A short film of Smith performing the poem "Undertaker" won awards at the Sundance and San Francisco film festivals. A former Metro columnist for the *Boston Globe*, Smith teaches writing periodically and is now a columnist for *Ms.* magazine and the online magazine *Afazi*.

Daniel S. Solis started writing poetry at the age of five. He has been called the Poet Laureate of Albuquerque and is a two-time 'Burque Poetry Slam Champion as well as two-time Asheville and Southeastern Regional Individual Champion. He has been a part of two National Championship Poetry

Slam teams and is a four-time Boston individual slam champ. He is also a member of the Taos Poetry Circus Open Slam and a member of the winning duo in last year's Taos Heavyweight Tag Team poetry bout. Solis' work has appeared in *Revival: Spoken Word from Lollapalooza* and *SLAM: the Art of Competitive Poetry*. He is also featured prominently in the movie *SlamNation*. He is the author of two books of poetry, *the other thing* and *Confusion Song*, and one CD, *Demo Peligroso*. Solis has performed poetry in ensemble form with multiple poets and musicians for the last three years with the Albuquerque Experiment. The *Austin Chronicle* describes him as "a fearless presence, with a dedication that treats poetry as something surpassing mere entertainment."

Quincy Troupe Jr. was born in 1943 in New York City. He attended Grambling College and Los Angeles City College. His books of poetry include *Choruses: Poems* (Coffee House Press, 1999); *Avalanche: Poems* (1996); *Weather Reports: New and Selected Poems* (1991); *Skulls along the River* (1984); *Snake-Back Solos: Selected Poems 1969–1977* (1979), which received an American Book Award; and *Embryo Poems, 1967–1971* (1974). He is also the author of *Miles: The Autobiography* (1989), which received an American Book Award; *James Baldwin: The Legacy* (1989); and the memoir, *Miles and Me: A Memoir of Miles Davis* (2000). Troupe edited the anthology *Giant Talk: An Anthology of Third World Writing* (1975) and is a founding editor of *Confrontation: A Journal of Third World Literature and American Rag*. In 1991, he received the Peabody Award for co-producing and writing the radio show *The Miles Davis Radio Project*. Among his honors and awards are fellowships from the National Foundation for the Arts, the New York Foundation for the Arts, and a grant from the New York State Council on the Arts. He is Professor of Creative Writing and American Literature at the University of California, San Diego. Quincy lives in La Jolla, California, with his wife, Margaret.

Michael Warr served as the executive director of the Guild Complex in Chicago for the literary art center's first decade. His awards for poetry include a National Endowment for the Arts Fellowship and the Gwendolyn Brooks Significant Illinois Poet Award. He has been widely anthologized and is the author of the collection of poems *We Are All the Black Boy* (Tia Chucha Press).

Saul Williams's debut performance and featured poetry in the Trimark Pictures film *Slam*, which he cowrote and starred in, brought audiences to their feet across the world. It won the Grand Jury Prize at the Sundance Film Festival (1998) and the Camera d'Or at the Cannes Film Festival, along with the Audience Award for Best Picture and the World Distributors Award for Best Picture. Along with his co-star, Sonia Sohn, Saul was awarded the Perry Ellis Breakthrough Award by New York's Independent Film Project (IFP) and was also nominated for a Spirit Award for best performance. Songwriting has become Saul's latest endeavor. Saul's debut album, *Amethyst Rock Star* (American Recordings/Island Def Jam), co-produced by Saul and production maverick Rick Rubin, was voted album of the year by the *Times of London*, and has received rave reviews across the world. Saul has two books of poetry: *She* (MTV/ Pocketbooks), now in its fifth printing; and his first book, *The Seventh Octave*, (Moore Black Press). Saul's work is also featured in a number of poetry anthologies: *Listen Up!* (Ballantine), *Catch The Fire* (Putnam), *Slam* (Grove/Atlantic), and *In Defense of Mumia* (Harlem River Press).

Adam Tapia-Grassi and **Kevin M. Derrig** are high school students and participants of the Youth Speaks poetry program.

index

acknowledgments

A very special thank you to michelle, donald, lynne, dom, kathleen, jayme and jimmy, jeff, matt and jen and kyle, nick, david and deb and litt' davie, ron and dr. joann and emily rose, greg, tom and lisa, george and norma and laura and anna, marc, dick, william "bill" kelly, ken and laura, raycifer, rob, kevin and krista and ailee, mike and teri, mike k., regie, sarah, and all the students and faculty at beecher high school and joliet west high school.

Thank you for your unacknowledged role as editor, my publishing and teaching partner and teacher, ronald maruszak.

Thank you to marvin bell and his sage like patience and advice, jerry quickley for recognizing my own areas of ignorance and slowly dragging me up to speed, and terry jacobus for his enthusiasm and hard work in bringing together two "enemy camps" who were never that far apart.

Thank you to the owner of the mighty Green Mill Jazz Club, dave jemillo, for providing a home for the Slam.

Thank you to Poetry Slam Inc. and the Slam family for developing the art form and assisting in providing sources for the book.

Text

Todd Alcott: "Television" by Todd Alcott, reprinted by permission of the author. Sherman Alexie: "Defending Walt Whitman"; "Song of Ourself"; "The Totem Sonnets"; "Marriage"; and "Inside Dachau" reprinted from *The Summer of Black Widows* © 1996 by Sherman Alexie, by permission of Hanging Loose Press. Marvin Bell: "To Dorothy" and "To No One in Particular" © 2000 by Marvin Bell, reprinted with permission by Copper Canyon Press. Tara Betts: "Rock'n'Roll Be a Black Woman" © 2000 by Tara Betts, first published in *Poetry Slam* by Gary Mex Glazner (ed.), Manic D Press; and "A Mixed Message" by Tara Betts, reprinted by permission of the author. Roger Bonair-Agard: "how do we spell free-dom—the wensi alphabeti method" by Roger Bonair-Agard, reprinted by permission of the author; "...Naming and Other Christian Things" © 2000 by Roger Bonair-Agard, published in *Poetry Slam* by Gary Mex Glazner (ed.), Manic D Press. Michael R. Brown: "Ice Worm" © 1994 by Michael R. Brown. First published in *Falling Wallendas* by Michael R. Brown; Tia Chucha Press. Lisa Buscani: "Hemingway Afternoon" and "Sirens at the Mill" © 1992 by Lisa Buscani. First published in *Jangle* by Lisa Buscani; Tia Chucha Press. Regie Cabico: "Peter Meets the Wolf" © 2003 by Regie Cabico, appears courtesy of the author; "Hansel Tells Gretel of the Witch" © 1997 by Regie Cabico, appeared in *Red Brick Review* and *Columbia* (1997), reprinted by permission of the author. Andrei Codrescu: "Untitled" and "On Drunkenness" by Andrei Codrescu, reprinted by permission of the author. Billy Collins: "Introduction to Poetry" © 1988 by Billy Collins. First published by the University of Arkansas Press. Kevin Coval: "Hear O' Israel" by Kevin Coval, reprinted by permission of the author. Kevin M. Derrig: "First Period" by Kevin M. Derrig, reprinted by permission of the author. DJ Renegade: "48 Hours After You Left" by DJ Renegade, reprinted by permission of the author. Kent Foreman: "Chicago" by Kent Foreman, reprinted by permission of the author. Regie Gibson: "alchemy"; excerpt from "eulogy of jimi christ"; "funknawlegy"; "it's a teenage thang"; "prayer"; and "in the year i loved your mother" © 2001 by Regie Gibson. First published in *Storms Beneath the Skin* by Regie Gibson; EM Press. Celena Glenn: "The Hand Has Turned" by Celena Glenn, reprinted by permission of the author. Edward Hirsch: "I am Going to Start Living Like a Mystic" and "Ocean of Grass" by Edward Hirsch, reprinted by permission of the author; "Song" © 1998 by Edward Hirsch, first published in *For the Sleepwalkers* by Edward Hirsch, Carnegie Mellon University Press; "Burning of the Midnight Lamp" © 2000 by Edward Hirsch, first published in *On Love* by Edward Hirsch, Alfred A. Knopf. Chinaka Hodge: "Losing" by Chinaka Hodge, reprinted by permission of the author. Shane Koyczan: "Beethoven" by Shane Koyczan, reprinted by permission of the author. Bob Holman: "DisClaimer"; "Praise Poem for Slam: Why Slam Causes Pain and Is a Good Thing"; and "Performance Poem" © 1995 by Bob Holman. First published in *Aloud: Voices from the Nuyorican Poets Café* by Miguel Algarín and Bob Holman (eds.), Henry Holt & Company. Jean Howard: "Dancing in Your Mother's Skin" and "Dollmaker" © 1991 by Jean Howard. First published in *Dancing in Your Mother's Skin* by Jean Howard; Tia Chucha Press. Terry Jacobus: "So Edgar Allen Poe Was in this Car"; "I Hear There Are Poets Here"; and "Patience" © 2002 by Terry Jacobus. Published in *Taos Poetry Circus: The Nineties*. Michael Kadela: "XXX" and "LXXIV" © 2002 by Michael Kadela. First published in *1 Hundred Hiccups* by Michael Kadela; EM Press. Yusef Komunyakaa: "Anodyne" and "Blue Light Lounge Sutra for the Performance Poets at Harold Park Hotel" by Yusef Komunyakaa, reprinted by permission of the author. Sarah Maehl: "Three A.M." and "On Rain" by Sarah Maehl, reprinted by permission of the author. Taylor Mali: "How to Write a Political Poem" and "Like Lilly Like Wilson" by Taylor Mali, reprinted by permission of the author. Steve Marsh: "Belated Valentine: A Work in Progress" by Steve Marsh, reprinted by permission of the author. Jack McCarthy: "Careful What You Ask For" and "Cartalk: A Love Poem" © 2003 by Jack McCarthy. Published by EM Press. Jeffrey McDaniel: "The Passion Tree"; "Dear America"; "The Abandoned Factory of Sense" and "The Foxhole Manifesto" © 2003 by Jeffrey McDaniel. First published by Alibi Press. George David Miller: "Before I Read This Poem" © 2002 by George David Miller. First published by EM Press. Brenda Moossy: "What I Said to the Man Installing the Hot Tub" by Brenda Moossy, reprinted by permission of the author. Viggo Mortensen: "Weekends"; "Hillside"; "Keepsake"; "Lullaby"; "Matinee"; and "Untitled" © 2002 by Viggo Mortensen. First published in *Coincidence of Memory* by Viggo Mortensen; Perceval Press. Jerry Quickley: "Hip Hop Hollas" by Jerry Quickley, reprinted by permission of the author. Peter Rabbit: "The Fight Game" and "Sports Teams" © 2002 by Peter Rabbit. Published in *Taos Poetry Circus: The Nineties*. Luis J. Rodriguez: "Crossing Boundaries, Crossing Cultures: Poetry Performance, and the New American Revolution" © 1997 by Luis J. Rodriguez. First printed in *Another Chicago Magazine*, p. 32–33. Cin Salach: "worship" and "Evolution" by Cin Salach, reprinted by permission of the author. Beau Sia: "Howl" and "Love" by Beau Sia, reprinted by permission of the author. Marc Smith: "Cat on a Coffin"; "The Father Has Faded"; "Dusty Blues"; "Street Musician"; and "Pull the Next One Up" © 1996 by Marc Smith. First published in *Crowdpleaser* by Marc Smith; Collage Press. Patricia Smith: "And Then She"; "Building Nicole's Mama"; "My Mother Learns English"; and "A Motherfucker Too" by Patricia Smith, reprinted by permission of the author. Daniel S. Solis: "Welcome to the Revolution" and "Elephant Song" by Daniel S. Solis, reprinted by permission of the author. Adam Tapia-Grassi: excerpt from "Guilt" by Adam Tapia-Grassi, reprinted by permission of the author. Quincy Troupe, Jr.: "Poem for the Root Doctor of Rock n Roll" and "Chicago: © 2002 by Quincy Troupe, Jr. Published by Coffee House Press. Michael Warr: "Low Down in the Get Me High Lounge" © 1991 by Michael Warr. First published in *We Are All the Black Boy* by Michael Warr; Tia Chucha Press. Saul Williams: "Amethyst Rocks" © 1997 by Saul Williams. First published in *The Seventh Octave* by Saul Williams; Moore Black Press.

Audio

Todd Alcott: "Television" by Todd Alcott appears courtesy of the author. Marvin Bell: "To Dorothy" by Marvin Bell appears courtesy of the author. Roger Bonair-Agard: "how do we spell freedom—the weusi alphabeti method" by Roger Bonair-Agard appears courtesy of the author. Billy Collins: "Introduction to Poetry" by Billy Collins appears courtesy of the author. Kevin M. Derrig: "First Period" by Kevin M. Derrig appears courtesy of the author. Sage Francis: "Beat Box Monster" by Sage Francis appears courtesy of the author. Regie Gibson: "It's a Teenage Thang" and "Amens" by Regie Gibson appear courtesy of the author. Celena Glenn: "The Hand Has Turned" and "Running a Race (No One Knows)" (performed by NYC-Urbana Slam Team) by Celena Glenn appear courtesy of the author. Edward Hirsch: "Song" by Edward Hirsch appears courtesy of the author. Bob Holman: "DisClaimer" by Bob Holman appears courtesy of the author. Terry Jacobus: "So Edgar Allan Poe Was in this Car" by Terry Jacobus appears courtesy of the author. Taylor Mali: "How to Write a Political Poem" by Taylor Mali appears courtesy of the author. Eli Marienthal: "Multiverse" by Eli Marienthal appears courtesy of the author. Jack McCarthy: "Careful What You Wish For" by Jack McCarthy appears courtesy of the author. Jeffrey McDaniel: "The Foxhole Manifesto" by Jeffrey McDaniel appears courtesy of the author. Brenda Moossy: "What I Said to the Man Installing the Hot Tub" by Brenda Moossy appears courtesy of the author. Viggo Mortensen: "Weekends" by Viggo Mortensen appears courtesy of the author. Jerry Quickley: "Hip Hop Hollas" by Jerry Quickley appears courtesy of the author. Cin Salach: "Music Swims Back to Me" (performed by Cin Salach and Ten Tongues) by Anne Sexton appears courtesy of Sterling Lord Literistic. Marc Smith: "Stupid Song"; "It"; "Slam Schtick"; and "Pull the Next One Up" by Marc Smith appear courtesy of the author. Patricia Smith: "A Motherfucker Too" by Patricia Smith appears courtesy of the author. Quincy Troupe, Jr.: "Chicago" by Quincy Troupe, Jr. appears courtesy of the author. Two Tongues: "Mother" by Two Tongues appears courtesy of the authors. Saul Williams: "Amethyst Rocks" by Saul Williams appears courtesy of the author.

Photos

All credits listed by page number. Every effort has been made to correctly attribute all the materials reproduced in this book. If any errors have been made, we will be happy to correct them in future editions.

4 Billy Collins; 9, 28 Marvin Bell; 52 Kevin Coval; 82–84, 92 Terry Jacobus; 87 Al Simmons; 95 Peter Rabbit; 178, 180 Beau Sia; 188 Patricia Smith; 196 Roger Bonair-Agard; 207 Lynn Stewart; photos on pages 7, 31, 41, 50, 57, 97, 106, and 183 appear courtesy of David Huang; photos on pages 26, 37, 39, 46, 59, 61, 77, 115, 120, 128, 132, 137, 138, 146–49, 152, 156, 201, 203, 211, 214, and 219 appear courtesy of Eric Ivan Plese; photos of Chicago street scenes appear courtesy of Megan Dempster.